WHEN GOD DOESN'T FIX IT

LAURA STORY

WITH KEVIN AND SHERRY HARNEY

WHEN GOD DOESN'T FIX IT

LEARNING TO WALK IN GOD'S PLANS
INSTEAD OF OUR OWN

STUDY GUIDE

FIVE SESSIONS

W Publishing Group

An Imprint of Thomas Nelson

thomasnelson.com

When God Doesn't Fix It Study Guide

Published in Nashville, Tennessee, by W Publishing Group, an imprint of Thomas Nelson. W Publishing Group and Thomas Nelson are registered trademarks of HarperCollins Christian Publishing, Inc.

Published in association with Creative Trust Literary Group, www.creativetrust.com, 201 Jamestown Park Dr. STE 200, Brentwood, TN 37027.

Thomas Nelson, Inc. titles may be purchased in bulk for educational, business, fund-raising, or sales promotional use. For information, please e-mail SpecialMarkets@ThomasNelson.com.

ISBN: 978-0-310-08916-2

First Printing February 2016 / Printed in the United States of America

Nov-02-2018 13885201810_WB_C

Contents

INTRODUCTION

Happily Ever After, After

Unexpected phone calls can be good or bad. But regardless of whether the content of the phone call is good or bad, it has the potential to change our lives in profound ways.

When the caller tells us the cancer is gone, that we've been hired, that there is a buyer for the house we're selling, or a thousand other good things, we immediately recognize the potential for change. In those moments, we're convinced the old life as we've known it is over and a breathtaking new one has just begun. Our hope soars, and we can't wait to get started! But when the call brings bad news, we don't want our life to change. In the midst of a tragedy, we just want everything to return to "normal" or "the way it used to be."

But is it possible that good things can come out of broken dreams? Is it conceivable that in the months that follow that initial frightening phone call, the possibility exists for a deeper intimacy with God, a renewed love for our friends and family, a greater comprehension of the scarcity of time, or a thousand other unexpected gifts? If we knew those treasures only came from walking through the valley, would we willingly choose the path that took us there?

For centuries, children have grown up hearing stories that end with the words, "And they lived happily ever after." With the advent of media-on-demand, endless production of animated Disney films, and the fairy princess motif running through so many cultural stories, it is easy for young people to conclude that their personal stories should end with these familiar words. Adding to the confusion is the message being communicated in many children's

Bible storybooks and Sunday school classes, in which a whole generation of kids has heard a message that gives the impression God promises to make all our dreams come true. If we do our best to follow Jesus, he will make sure we experience smooth sailing through this life and into the next.

But God does not promise a painless and easy life this side of eternity, nor does the Bible guarantee endless delight and overflowing blessing every step of our journey. We are not assured of a "happily ever after" exclamation at the end of our years on this planet. Let's be clear: God loves his children. He delights to bless his people, and his grace is always present and sufficient. But he does not promise a painless, struggle-free, easy path through this life. What he guarantees is to be with us every step of the journey.

This world is not our home and it is certainly not our eternal destination. God has something even better planned for his beloved children. This life will have loss, heartache, struggle, and pain. When we walk with Jesus we will also drink in amazing joy, deep love, stunning beauty, and peace in the storms. And, when it is all said and done, we will find out that every person who travels through life hand-in-hand with Jesus will live happily ever after, after this life when we see Jesus face-to-face.

How to Use This Guide

The *When God Doesn't Fix It* video study is designed to be experienced in a group setting such as a Bible study, Sunday school class, or any small group gathering. Each session begins with a brief "talk about it" question to get you and the group engaged and thinking about the topic. You will then watch the video with Laura Story and jump into some directed small-group Bible study and discussion questions. Even though there are many questions available for your small group, don't feel that you have to use them all. Your leader will focus on the ones that resonate most with your group and guide you from there.

Each person in the group should have his or her own study guide, which includes video notes, small-group discussion questions, and daily personal studies to deepen learning between sessions. Participants are also strongly encouraged to have a copy of the *When God Doesn't Fix It* book. Reading the book alongside the curriculum provides even deeper insights that make the journey richer and more meaningful.

It's going to be great! However, if you want to get the most out of your experience, you need to keep a couple of things in mind. First, note that the real growth in this study will happen during your small-group time. This is where you will process the content of Laura's message, ask questions, and learn from others as you listen to what God is doing in their lives. For this reason, it is important to be committed to the group and attend each session so you can build trust and rapport with the other members of your group.

Second, remember that as much as small groups can be a deeply rewarding time of intimacy and friendship, they can also be a disaster. Work to make your group a "safe place." That means first being honest about your thoughts and feelings as well as listening carefully to everyone else's opinion. (**Note:** If you are a group leader, there are additional instructions and resources in the back of the book for leading a productive discussion group.)

Third, resist the temptation to "fix" a problem someone might be having or to correct his or her theology. That's not what this time is for. In addition, make sure you keep everything your group shares confidential. All this will foster a rewarding sense of community in your small group and give God's Spirit some space to heal, challenge, and engineer life transformation.

Following your group time, you can maximize the impact of the course with additional study between the sessions. For each session, you may wish to complete the personal study all in one sitting or to spread it out over a few days (for example, working on it a half-hour a day on five different days that week). Note that if you are unable to finish (or even start!) your between-sessions personal study, still attend the group study video session. We are all busy, and life happens. You are still wanted and welcome at the group even if you don't have your "homework" done.

Keep in mind this is an opportunity to train in a new way of seeing the world. The videos, discussions, and studies are simply meant to kick-start your imagination to help you see how God is working through the troubled times and be a willing partner with him in his plan. As you do so, you will find hope in the midst of ongoing tragedy, healing in brokenness, peace in raging storms, and priceless gifts even in unresolved circumstances.

Of Note: The quotations interspersed throughout this study guide and the introductory comments are excerpts from the book ***When God Doesn't Fix It*** and the video curriculum of the same name by Laura Story. The in-between sessions material is by Laura Story with Jennifer Schuchmann. All other resources have been written by Kevin and Sherry Harney.

SESSION ONE

Don't Be Surprised by Trouble

Our hope comes in Jesus, even when he doesn't do what we want him to do. Even when he doesn't fix what's broken in our life. . . . When Jesus is with us, he's our anchor in the rough waters of a troubled life. If we want to survive the storm we need to cling to him like the salvation he is.

LAURA STORY

Introduction

There is a popular expression that says, "Into each life some rain must fall." We all encounter stormy times in our lives. Sometimes this takes the form of just a gentle rain, but at other times it is an intense downpour with hurricane-force winds. When these times come, it is difficult for us not to be taken back and ask, *God, why did this happen?*

Perhaps what we need to do is adopt the mindset of a young boy named Daniel. Daniel grew up in a tough neighborhood. He had friends whose houses were robbed, and he knew that if he left his bike out front at night, there was a good chance it would be gone in the morning. He knew better than to walk around his block alone after dark. He was on his toes when he saw strangers and was ready to run home as fast as he could if he sensed trouble.

Would you say that Daniel was *paranoid* or *prepared*?

The truth is, Daniel sees the world he lives in the way it really is. He has learned that he should be prepared, careful, and aware of his surroundings. Daniel has his eyes open to the fact that this world can be a dangerous place and the neighborhood where he lives has very specific hazards. His preparedness actually makes his neighborhood a safer place for him.

> Dear friends, do not be surprised at the fiery ordeal that has come on you to test you, as though something strange were happening to you. But rejoice inasmuch as you participate in the sufferings of Christ, so that you may be overjoyed when his glory is revealed (1 Peter 4:12–13).

If Daniel did not recognize the risks around him, or if he decided to ignore them, he would be in greater danger. But by honestly looking at the threats in the environment where he lives, he can make decisions and take actions that help him make it through each day. As believers in Christ, we need to do the same. We need to take to heart

Jesus' words when he said, "In this world you will have trouble." But we must also remember the rest of that verse: "But take heart! I have overcome the world" (John 16:33).

Talk About It

Welcome to the first session of *When God Doesn't Fix It*. If you or any of your fellow group members do not know one another, take some time to introduce yourselves. Next, to get things started, discuss one of the following questions:

- What are some beliefs you held as a child that turned out not to be true? How do the misconceptions we hold as children often shape our lives?

or

- How can the recognition that this life will have loss, pain, and trouble prepare us to face these challenging times? What are some of the consequences if we deny or ignore the reality of pain in this life?

Video Teaching Notes

As you watch the video teaching segment for session one, use the following outline to record anything that stands out to you.

Trouble finds its way into our lives

When hard truth comes crashing in

A new understanding of the biblical story

The good news of the gospel:

- The reality and cost of sin

- The gift of grace (God's love revealed through Jesus)

- The glory of eternal life

Man chose to disobey God and the result was a marring of creation that could only be rectified by the sacrifice of a loving Savior.

The cost of following Jesus

Standing on the solid rock

Bible Study and Video Discussion

Take a few minutes with your group members to discuss what you just watched and explore these concepts in Scripture.

1. Many people grow up believing or being taught that God promises to give us a good, safe, pain-free life if we do our best to follow and honor him. What were you taught or led to believe about how God will treat you if you seek to live a good life for him? Where do you think this teaching came from?

The older I get, the more I learn that the pursuit of truth is a lifelong endeavor.

2. In the story of Daniel, we read how God closed the mouths of lions and allowed him to walk out of the den unscratched. In the story of David, we see how the giant Goliath fell defeated at his feet. What is the danger of simplifying Bible stories like these into lessons that give the impression that people of faith always end up on top and win the earthly battles they face? What are other Bible stories that are often used in a way that sends this message to children and adults?

3. The truth is that few characters in the Bible were so good that their behavior warranted God's unquestioning blessing.

Who are some characters in the Bible who had both good and bad qualities? How does the presence of so many biblical characters with a mix of good and bad affirm that God's blessings in our life are not based on our "good behavior"?

Our hope isn't found in being good so God will be good to us. Our hope is found in the person of Jesus Christ, his overwhelming love for us, and his ability to sustain us no matter what this life brings.

4. Read **Romans 6:19–23.** What do you learn in this passage about the battle between sin and righteousness? According to Paul, what are the consequences of sin? How do you see this reality in our world today?

What are the results of becoming a "slave" to God? What benefits do we gain from living a life of holiness?

5. Read **Romans 5:12.** Why is it absolutely essential that we understand the bad news of sin if we are going to fully understand the good news of the gospel and the hope we have in Jesus? If someone looked at you and said, "I don't think sin is really a big deal," what would you say to help him or her understand the extent and cost of sin?

6. Read **Romans 3:23**, **Ephesians 2:8–9**, and **Romans 8:1–4.** How is salvation a gift to be received and not a payment to be earned? What is the danger of believing that our actions and "goodness" are the reason for our salvation?

Despite what culture tells us, Scripture states clearly that the way to know eternal life is through the person of Jesus Christ.

7. How does a relationship with Jesus and the hope of eternal life help you stand strong during the storms you face in this life? What is a tough time you recently walked through? How has your relationship with Jesus enabled you to stand strong and endure?

8. Read **2 Corinthians 4:16–18.** What does the apostle Paul mean when he says, "Our light and momentary troubles are achieving for us an eternal glory that far outweighs them all"? How can we keep our eyes and focus on what is unseen and eternal as we walk through the hard times of this life?

For the disciples, following Jesus didn't lead to better homes or better jobs or more comfortable lives. It led the majority of these men to their deaths, but not before experiencing the kind of life worth dying for.

9. Read **2 Corinthians 11:16–33.** What are some of the struggles, pains, and losses the apostle Paul faced as he lived for Jesus? How could he be so optimistic and joy-filled in light of all he suffered?

10. How can your group members pray for you and support you as you walk through a painful time or as you support someone you love who is going through a difficult time?

In our search for truth, is it possible that God, in his sovereignty, might allow the things in life that appear to be sturdy to lose their sturdiness, in order to show us that Jesus truly is the only sturdy thing in this life?

Closing Prayer

Use the prompts below to guide your group in a time of prayer together:

- Thank God for those people who taught you the Bible and instructed you in the truth of God's Word.
- Praise God for the times he has delivered you from the lions' den and given you power to overcome giants—and also praise him for the power he gives to stand in faith even when the battles you face don't have a happy ending.
- Celebrate the amazing and undeserved gift of grace revealed in the death of Jesus for your sins.
- Ask God to teach you to walk in joy even during the storms of life.
- Pray for group members to cling to Jesus with deep faith for as long as they walk through the valley of pain and loss . . . even if it takes a lifetime.

Between-Sessions
PERSONAL STUDY

Reflect on the content covered in this first session by exploring the following material from the Bible and from *When God Doesn't Fix It.* Before you begin, answer these questions:

What are you hoping to gain from this study?

What are some difficult situations that you are facing right now?

What questions do you have for God about these situations?

What do you feel God is teaching you through these circumstances?

Day One: The Reality of Our World

In the video this week, Laura shared about some of the symptoms her husband, Martin, began to experience after they moved to Atlanta. For several months he had been more forgetful than usual, but now he began to seem perpetually exhausted. At first Laura thought it was because of his hectic work and school schedule, but soon he started falling asleep during Bible studies or—even worse—during worship services at Perimeter Church.

Martin had been a go-getter with tons of energy, but soon he began falling asleep at social events. For Laura, he had become someone she didn't recognize. Ultimately, the doctors diagnosed the cause of Martin's symptoms: a brain tumor. This life-changing event shook Laura and caused her to reassess the beliefs she had held about God since she was a child. These were beliefs such as if she followed Jesus and was the "best" Christian she could be, God would reward her with a pain-free life. But Laura came to understand that God didn't owe her anything—and that she could never be "good enough" to earn God's blessings. As Isaiah wrote, "All of us have become like one who is unclean, and all our righteous acts are like filthy rags (64:6)."

But the question remains: *Why does life have to be so hard?* Paul summed up the reason in Romans 5:12: "Just as sin entered the world through one man, and death through sin . . . in this way death came to all people, because all sinned." Our world is decaying—seen in the form of death, addiction, adultery—because *sin* entered our world. In fact, when we look at the story of the Bible, we find the narrative breaks down into four parts: creation, fall, redemption, and restoration. Understanding these four segments of the narrative, and where we fall within them, will give us insight into what we can expect not only from God but also from ourselves.

1. Read **John 16:33.** What does Jesus say our lives will involve here on earth? What promise does he give to us?

2. Read **Romans 5:18–19.** What does Paul say are the effects of sin entering into the world? How are people made righteous again?

3. Given these passages, why is it unrealistic to expect that we will not have trials in life—regardless of how "good" we think we are before God? Why should we expect trouble?

Day Two: God's Perfect Creation

How did we come into being? How did the world come to be? You've probably asked those and similar questions—and by now, you've likely arrived at an answer. Whether in church, or in a science class, you've heard one or more explanations of how the earth was created, and you've chosen which one you believe. If you accept what is taught in the Bible, you believe the world was created by an all-knowing, all-powerful, and all-loving God. God, the Creator of the universe, was there before time began and will be there when time ends.

He was. And is. And will always be.

Some argue whether God created the world in a literal six days or whether he allowed it to evolve over several millions of years. But more important than exactly *how* it was created is the truth that "in the beginning *God* created the heavens and the earth" (Genesis 1:1, emphasis added). The earth was beautiful. And good. It was a tropical paradise lit by a brilliant, yellow sun and cooled by deep, blue pools of water. Every animal flourished in harmony with each other and with the humans God created to oversee them all. Peace and purpose reigned.

The pinnacle of God's creation was a man named Adam and a woman named Eve. God created them to worship, love, and serve him. "God created mankind in his own image, in the image of God he created them; male and female he created them" (Genesis 1:27). More than anything, God wanted a relationship with Adam and Eve, and he gave them free will so they could do those things freely and voluntarily. And for a while, they did.

The Lord put Adam into the Garden of Eden to work it and take care of it. Together, he, Eve, and God would walk through the garden. They would stop to pet the lion that had lain down with the lambs. In that perfect Eden, Adam and Eve were free to do whatever they chose—with one exception. God warned them not to eat the fruit off of one particular tree—the tree of the knowledge of good and evil—which stood in the center of the garden.

When Adam and Eve disobeyed God's command, it ushered in the next section of the Bible's narrative: sin and the fall.

1. Read **Genesis 2:5–17.** How would you describe the earth based on this account?

2. What task did God give Adam to do in the garden? What freedoms did God give him? What restrictions were imposed?

3. What did God say would be the consequences of Adam's disobedience?

Day Three: Sin Enters the World

"When the woman saw that the fruit of the tree was good for food and pleasing to the eye, and also desirable for gaining wisdom, she took some and ate it. She also gave some to her husband, who was with her, and he ate it" (Genesis 3:6). So it was that Adam and Eve disregarded God's instruction. There was a lot of temptation and blame to throw around, but in the end they broke the one rule God had given them and ate fruit from the forbidden tree.

Despite what Adam and Eve thought (or perhaps what they hoped), the created could never hope to be equal to the Creator. Though they had dominion over all creation, and though God had given them freedom to make their own decisions and rule the earth, Adam and Eve had no right to disregard the Lord's rule. When they did, the consequences of their rebellion were real and swift.

Immediately, they realized they were naked and hid in shame. They were forced to leave the peace and serenity of the Garden of Eden and were not allowed to return. For the first time they had to scrounge for food, as their once-ample supply was now gone. They developed a taste for meat. Animals and humans would no longer be safe mixing with those that weren't the same species. Eve gave birth to children, and it was painful. The children fought, and eventually one son killed the other. Sickness and disease entered the world. What was once healthy, and eternal, began to decay. Death followed.

The consequences of Adam and Eve's sin is a tidal wave that has continued to knock down every generation in its path. The world God made is no longer at peace, and nothing is in the same condition as when he created it. People don't act like they should. The result of sin is on the front page of every newspaper, as well as the eleven o'clock news. All around us, we observe broken lives, broken treaties, broken promises, and broken relationships. We ourselves are treading in the stinky, murky, dark, dirty waters of our own making, hoping not to go under.

The biggest break is our relationship with God. And yet, rather than repair it, we continue the rebellion through our lies and grudges, holding on to anger, and lusting over people and things we prefer to keep private. We hold hate in our hearts and envy in our eyes. We lust, we leak, we fumble, and we fail. "There is no one righteous, not even one; there is no one who understands; there is no one who seeks God. All have turned away, they have together become worthless; there is no one who does good, not even one" (Romans 3:11–12).

It's called the "fall" because we've fallen away from God, and we can't get up by ourselves. Everything is distorted and broken, and as much as we try, we can't put our humpty-dumpty world back together again. But fortunately, God did not leave us in this state. Even as he uttered the curse against humankind, he was planning a way for each of us to be reconciled. God's plan would usher in the next section of the Bible's narrative: redemption.

1. Read **Genesis 3:6–10.** What were the immediate effects of Adam and Eve's disobedience?

2. Read **Genesis 3:11–19.** What were the long-term effects of their sin (the curse)?

3. What are some of the consequences of the fall that you see today?

Day Four: Restoring the Broken

In our broken world, each of us has a plan to fix the things we see are broken. Maybe, for you, the answer is a political party, an ideology, or a philosophy. Perhaps it is a self-help book or a person you idolize. We believe that if everyone would just see things the way *we* do—do what we tell them to do—everything would be okay. The problem is that none of us can agree on what that plan should be.

Whenever we try to integrate our solution, we reach a point where we can't take it any further. As much as we'd like, *we don't rule the world,* because we didn't create it. So we fail at our attempts to spread our personal gospel of solutions—yet somehow, we each believe there is *someone* or *something* that can make things right. We can agree there is a rescuer, even if we can't agree on who or what it is.

And we are right. There is a rescuer. Even though God hated our sin and rebellion, he determined to restore his relationship with us. Ever since Adam and Eve messed up, God has had a plan to restore us. He even promised Adam and Eve there would be a rescue. He said one of their descendants would crush the evil that had been unloosed on the earth.

Through the generations, God's plan continued to unfold. Centuries before the rescuer's coming, the prophets dropped hints about his birth, life, and death. They recorded these accounts and passed them down in both oral and written form. In these accounts, which we have assembled into sacred Scripture, we learn he would live the perfect and blameless life we were intended to live—and that our punishment would become his.

The entire record, gathered into what we today call the Old Testament, points to this rescuer and this climactic event that would occur in history. And then it did. Jesus Christ, the Son of God, entered history as a baby born in Bethlehem. This God-man spent his life helping those around him understand what these ancient eyewitness accounts meant when they alluded to him. He interpreted them and prophesied about his own death and resurrection. He directed people to his loving Father. And though he lived a blameless and perfect life, as part of his Father's plan, he agreed to take the punishment for our sins—past, present, and future.

Our faith in Christ's ability to rescue us relieves us of the punishment we are due and restores our relationship with his Father—God, our Creator. For all those who believe Jesus is their rescuer, his death and resurrection overcomes our sin and its consequences. He overcomes physical death and restores eternal life. "The Lord Jesus Christ, who gave himself for our sins to rescue us from the present evil age, according to the will of our God and Father, to whom be glory for ever and ever" (Galatians 1:3–5).

Outside of Jesus, we cannot restore our relationship with God or our broken world. We can't stop sin or the consequences of sin from happening. But with our faith in God's plan and in Jesus whom he sent to rescue us, we can now turn from our rebellious ways and have victory over sin. But the story doesn't end there, for God promises to renew the whole world. This is the final section of the Bible's narrative: *restoration*.

1. Read **2 Corinthians 5:17–21.** What does Paul say God sent Jesus into this world to do? What happens to us when we accept Christ as our rescuer?

2. Now that we have been reconciled to God, what does the Lord command us to do? What does it mean to be an "ambassador" for Christ?

3. Read **Hebrews 10:10.** What does it mean that Christ paid the price for our sins once and for all time?

Day Five: A New Heaven and Earth

In the book of Revelation, we read how Christ will one day return to judge sin and evil and escort in righteousness and peace. The disciple John gives us a glimpse of what this glorious new heaven and new earth will look like. He also writes that at this time, "[God] will wipe every tear. . . . There will be no more death or mourning or crying or pain, for the old order of things has passed away" (Revelation 21:4).

Perhaps you have your own vision of what this new reality will be like. Picture the world as you've always wanted it, with no more earthquakes, tornados, tsunamis, or hurricanes. No more wars, guns, hate, or aggression. A place where people aren't defined by their race, gender, or physical limitations. No more sickness and no more cancer. No more broken hearts. A place where family members can no longer hurt you, where bosses won't lie and cheat, and where gossiping friends cease. Broken things will be completely fixed. No more selfishness and no more divorce.

For the first time, you'll feel whole. You will be complete. You'll never fight or argue again. The things you long for most—love, security, joy, meaning, and purpose—will be abundant. Death, decay, and destruction will be gone. Peace and love will prevail. Humans and animals will once more live together in harmony. The world will be perfect, the way God intended it to be.

All of the good things we desire will be present, but this won't be a utopia with us at the center of it. Though we all have a shared vision for this perfect world, at the center of it will be Jesus to whom all praise, glory, and honor belong. We will worship him. We will serve him. And we will be in perfect relationship with him for eternity.

Until then, even though we've been rescued, we still feel the consequences of the original fall. We still deal with unexpected troubles and pain because we are still living in a fallen world. But because we've been rescued, we know that Jesus is our anchor in the rough waters of a troubled life. We can survive the storm by clinging to him like the salvation he is. And when we're with him, we can be a part of the restoration.

It starts with us restoring our relationship with our heavenly Father. With us recognizing that as people who are rescued and who know the rescuer, we can help others escape their own sin cages. With us understanding that our job, our purpose, is to help reveal God's coming perfect world for others to glimpse before it is ushered in completely. And as we serve God, love Jesus, and respond to the Holy Spirit's whispers in our lives, we can heal ourselves and begin to give others a glimpse of what life looks like when what's broken is fixed. Together, we can begin to work for the world that we all desire.

1. Read **Revelation 21:1–5.** How does John describe the new heaven and new earth?

2. How do you picture the restoration that God promises to provide?

3. How can you help give others a glimpse now of what this restoration will look like?

SESSION TWO

Best-Made Plans

We each have plans and dreams for our lives. We think we know what's best and if God just followed our plan, everything would be great. But God's plans are much bigger than ours. . . . When we trust that God is for us and not against us, we can see our future as he sees it. It is a future filled with plans to prosper you and not to harm you. Plans to give you hope and a future. And plans that will ultimately draw you closer to him.

LAURA STORY

Introduction

Joni Eareckson Tada was a teenager going out for a swim when her life was radically changed. A diving accident left her a quadriplegic in a wheelchair. This was not the plan she had for her life. Nonetheless, today she inspires people around the world with paintings she does by holding a brush in her teeth, by sharing how her faith continues to carry her through the challenges she faces, and by leading a ministry for people with disabilities.

Christine Caine knew nothing about human trafficking. She was not a crusader, but she was a faithful follower of Jesus. She did not have plans to begin a ministry or go to war against an international practice of injustice and human degradation. But God redirected her steps and reordered her life. Christine Caine now travels the world battling against the practice of selling human beings as objects.

Ann Voskamp never aspired to be a public speaker. She had no grand goals to travel around the world and talk about faith, thankfulness, or any other topic. As a matter of fact, she is not fond of getting on planes and flying anywhere. If the decision had been up to Ann to design her days, she would have stayed on the family farm, taught her children, loved her husband, and wrote her thoughts out in private journals. But God did not check in with Ann about his plan for her life. He called her, inspired her, and gave her a message. She wrote it down in her book *One Thousand Gifts*. Her life has now taken a trajectory she did not ask for and did not plan for—but one that God designed for her.

What is it God might be calling you to let go of, to leave behind, in order to take hold of a greater blessing?

What do all three of these women have in common? None of them planned where they are today. How could they have? But each would tell you that somehow, in his sovereignty, God has led them in ways that have brought him glory and led to true and lasting joy.

Talk About It

To get things started for this second session, discuss one of the following questions:

- When you were younger and dreamed of what a "perfect life" would look like for you, what pictures and future did you imagine? How is your life today different than you thought it might be?

or

- When you were a child, what did you think you would "be" when you grew up? How has God led you toward or away from that childhood sense of what your future would hold?

Video Teaching Notes

As you watch the video teaching segment for session two, use the following outline to record anything that stands out to you.

The perfectly planned life and the reality of detours

How we respond when God calls us to follow his plans and not our own

What role does our faith play in how tightly we hold on to "our plans"?

The story of Abraham and Sarah:

- The purpose of biblical stories

living & active
sharper than 2 edged sword
submit ourselves to the scripture

- God's call on Abraham and Sarah

- The call can be surprising and difficult

Abraham's faith journey had highs and lows. He believed God's promises from a young age, yet he got out into the real world and struggled to trust those promises in the midst of hard seasons. He was a lot like you and me.

Martin and Laura's journey

Other stories of faithfully following through during challenging times

God's plan for your life is about the journey, the process, the relationship of faith that is built with every shaky step.

Where is God calling us and what do we need to let go of to follow him well?

Bible Study and Video Discussion

Take a few minutes with your group members to discuss what you just watched and explore these concepts in Scripture.

1. Think about a time you experienced a significant detour away from how you had planned your future. As you look back, how was God directing your path through this detour?

The question isn't whether our lives will turn out like the glorious plans we've made. The question is how will we respond when they don't.

2. In the video, Laura talks about how some dreams in life can become broken and painful longings—such as the woman who desires to be married but can't seem to meet the right man, or the couple who longs for a child but faces infertility, or the woman who loves life but faces health challenges that limit her abilities and threaten her future. Think about a time you faced a significant and painful detour that brought about a longing in your life. How did you respond, both good and bad, when you faced this situation?

3. How can the way we respond to painful detours strengthen our faith? How can it damage our relationship with Jesus?

4. **Read Genesis 11:27–12:9** and **Genesis 15:1–6.** What do you learn about Abraham and Sarah and the detours and challenges they faced as you read these passages?

5. What do you learn about God and his ways as you read the story of Abraham and Sarah? How do you see the character of God at work in your life in similar ways to what this ancient couple experienced?

Is it possible that the very God who loved us enough
to give his only Son for us has a greater plan for our lives
than even we could dream up?

6. Think about a person in your life who has followed Jesus closely, faced painful detours, and held on to Jesus through the loss, pain, and struggles. What have you learned from the example and journey of this person?

7. Think about a time when God called you to give something up, leave something behind, and move forward to follow his will for your life. How did you respond to his call? What have you learned through this experience?

We don't just read the Scriptures for some tips on living or
a spiritual pep talk. We submit ourselves to the Scriptures,
asking God to use his Word to transform our lives.

8. In the video, Laura noted that God often shows us more about what we are leaving and giving up than he does about where we

are going. How have you experienced this in your journey? Why do you think God does not feel compelled to spell out exactly where he is taking you and what lies ahead as you follow him?

9. Martin and Laura did not really discover why God led them to Atlanta and Perimeter Bible Church until after the fact. Think about a time when you looked back, after a considerable journey, and finally saw the wisdom of where God had taken you. What would you have missed out on if you had fought God and not followed his plan?

10. How do you respond to this statement: "God is as concerned about the journey, process, and our faith along the way as he is about the actual destination"?

11. Think about one area of your life in which you sense God might be calling you to let go of something and follow him more fully. What is getting in the way of you stepping out and following God passionately into this adventure?

Just as we see in Abraham's life, our "going" usually is preceded by some level of "letting go."

12. How can your group members pray for you, encourage you, and support you as you seek God for the power to let go of what you must release so you can fully follow his plan for your future in this specific area of your life?

It's in the letting go of this world that we find God's best plans for us—when we place our trust in the One who vows to never let go of us.

Closing Prayer

Use the prompts below to guide your group in a time of prayer together:

- Thank God for the detours you have faced that have led you closer to him.
- Pray for strength and humility as you follow God through the situations that still don't make sense or show any signs of resolution.

- Invite God to surprise you with new life direction that is in line with his will, even if it does not line up with your plans.

- Lift up group members who are going through a hard season. Pray for God's presence, for his power to help them follow well, and for his will to be revealed in their lives.

- Thank God for people in your life who have been, or who continue to be, amazing examples of following God through the storms and struggles of life.

Between-Sessions
PERSONAL STUDY

Reflect on the content covered in this second session by exploring the following material from the Bible and from *When God Doesn't Fix It.*

Day One: Fuzzy Details

In the video this week, Laura noted that when she and Martin made plans to move to Atlanta, they thought it would be for just a few years. Laura imagined Martin would complete his degree in design, she would serve as the worship leader at Perimeter Church, and then they would move to South Carolina to be near their parents. This was their plan for a perfect life. However, God's plans for them would prove to be very different. Along the way, they would go through some hard seasons that would test them and make them wonder where God was leading.

This week, you read a bit about a couple in the Bible who had also made plans. God selected a man named Abraham to lead a nation of his chosen people. But to be that leader, Abraham had to leave his life as he knew it. "The Lord had said to Abram, 'Go from your country, your people and your father's household to the land I will show you'" (Genesis 12:1).

It's interesting that God said *go* but didn't tell Abraham *where* to go. Even more interesting, God made it clear what Abraham was to depart from—his country, his people, and his family. When he did this, God made Abraham a promise: "I will make you into a great nation, and I will bless you; I will make your name great, and you will be a blessing. I will bless those who bless you, and whoever curses you I will curse; and all peoples on earth will be blessed through you" (Genesis 12:2–3).

There's a problem, though. In the next verse, we find out that Abraham was *seventy-five* years old. That's a little old to be a father of an *infant*, let alone of a *multitude*. But Abraham does as he's told and ends up in Canaan. Yet there's another problem: Canaan is occupied. It was a bit like God promising you a dream house but when you roll up, you find the Taliban living in it. Oddly, God was specific about what Abraham was leaving behind and about the blessings he was going to give him, but God was sketchy on the details of the new country.

Why would God do that? Was he trying to hide something from Abraham? Or trick him? Or could it be that if Abraham had known what was in store for him, he wouldn't have left his father's house?

As Laura shared in the video this week, if God had told her that she and Martin were moving to Atlanta indefinitely, she would have kicked and screamed the whole way there. But God wanted them in Atlanta because that's where they needed to be to handle what happened next. If God hadn't kept the details from them, they might have missed out on the blessings that were theirs once they were obedient.

1. Read **Genesis 12:1–9.** What promises did God make to Abraham? What details did God provide about how those promises would be worked out?

2. In Romans 4:21, Paul writes that Abraham was "fully persuaded that God had power to do what he promised." Why do you think Abraham had such faith in God?

3. What would have happened if Abraham had stayed put? What can you learn from his example of following God even when all the details were not clear?

Day Two: Real People

It is clear that God wanted to rewrite the story of Abraham and Sarah's lives. He wanted to make the couple the head of a great nation. He also wanted to bless Abraham so that Abraham would be a blessing to others. After all, the blessings God gives aren't for us to use to grow fat and lazy but to serve and bless others. If you know the end of the story, you know that ultimately Abraham's lineage gave birth to Jesus, the promised Messiah. Abraham's blessings resulted in the *greatest* blessing we could ever receive: restoration with God.

Fortunately for us, Abraham trusted in God's promises even when it seemed the fulfillment of those promises was impossible. He trusted that somehow God would give him a son even though Sarah was barren and too old to have kids. However, this doesn't mean he was always a shining example of trusting in God in every situation. In fact, right after God called Abraham and gave him these incredible promises, we discover that Abraham was a bit of a liar.

Shortly after Abraham pitched his tent in Bethel, another unexpected situation arose: a famine broke out in the land. Once again, Abraham and Sarah were forced to change their plans, this time traveling down to Egypt where there was food. Once there, Abraham was asked if Sarah was his wife. "No, she's my sister," Abraham responded. While it was technically true that they shared a father, Abraham was lying to protect himself.

Despite Abraham's sin, God still promised to protect him and reward him for his faith. But Abraham was consumed by the fact he and Sarah didn't have children. Abraham had great wealth, but without children, a servant would inherit his fortune. Despite God's assurances that wouldn't happen, Abraham and Sarah grew tired of waiting on God. Here's a twenty-first century interpretation of what transpired:

One day, Sarah came to Abraham and reminded him that God had promised they would have a baby. It seems Sarah had come up with a great plan—she would have Abraham sleep with her young Egyptian maidservant, Hagar. I imagine Abraham pausing just long enough to make Sarah believe he had to really think about this idea before agreeing to take her up on the offer. Sarah's strategy would pay off nine months later when Hagar gave birth to an illegitimate son named Ishmael.

This is not to make light of what they did, because it was more than their just going outside of God's plan to have a baby. When they made that decision, they were also going outside of God's plan to be a blessing to others. These stories make us wonder what is up with this couple. Abraham lied and deceived others on several occasions. Sarah was impatient and created a lot of agony for her family by trying to intervene in God's plans. So why would God put up with them and continue to work in their lives?

In fact, that is just the point of these stories. Abraham and Sarah were real people with real sins, just like you and me. Sometimes they trusted God, and sometimes they took matters into their own hands. But the beauty of the story is that God was faithful to the couple even when they were unfaithful to him. God basically told Abraham there was not enough sin in the world for him to mess up his plan! Even his disobedience couldn't thwart God's agenda.

While God doesn't delight in our disobedience, he does delight in using broken, faithless people to showcase how faithful a God he is. That's great news for you and me. Despite our sins, we can't wreck God's plan. When we make a bad move, he's like a master chess player, resetting the board to show his goodness and grace.

1. Read **Genesis 12:10–20.** Why did Abraham come up with this scheme to say Sarah was his sister? In what ways does this reveal he wasn't trusting in God?

2. Read **Genesis 16:1–4.** Why did Sarah come up with this scheme? In what ways does this reveal that she wasn't trusting in God's promises?

3. How do these stories illustrate that Abraham and Sarah were real people with real failings, struggles, and doubts? How did God use them in spite of their failures?

Day Three: Another Curveball

Abraham and Sarah eventually did have the child that God had promised them. Isaac was the love of their lives, and they wanted to celebrate their new son without the shameful reminders of their past. So, ultimately, they expelled Hagar, the maidservant, and Ishmael from the region.

By this time the family had settled down in Beersheba. They had their fortune and, now, their long-awaited child. The dreams of their very lengthy lives had been fulfilled. Their world revolved around this little baby God promised. Abraham must have been feeling very comfortable in his covenant with God. His family was stable, and he had a new permanent address. Abraham would never have expected what happened next. We pick up the story in Genesis 22:

> Some time later God tested Abraham. He said to him, "Abraham!"
>
> "Here I am," he replied.
>
> Then God said, "Take your son, your only son, whom you love—Isaac—and go to the region of Moriah. Sacrifice him there as a burnt offering on a mountain I will show you" (verses 1–2).

Why did Abraham say, "Here I am"? Had God somehow misplaced Abraham? Or was he just curious about Abraham's geographical location? The text doesn't tell us, but because of what happens next, I think we can assume that Abraham had learned that when God called, he answered. So Abraham was metaphorically raising his hand, saying, "I'm right here, God. Whatever it is you're calling me to do, here I am to do it."

He might have also added, "And thanks for this cute little boy you've given us. He's just the sweetest thing ever, and I'm so in love with him!" If he didn't say it, he was probably thinking it. But then God gets specific and asks Abraham to take his son—his only son (and by *only* son God means Abraham's *favored legitimate* son)—and do something so troubling it is hard to believe a good God could even ask it. God wanted Abraham to sacrifice Isaac.

Just to be clear, that means God was asking him to *kill* or *murder* his own son as an offering to God. And if that wasn't clear enough, the language God used here is reminiscent of the language

God used when he asked Abraham to sacrifice his country, his people, and his father's house. There was no mistake about this.

Abraham knew exactly what God was asking. This wasn't an uncommon command in this culture. Many of the false gods that people worshiped demanded child sacrifices. But it was completely inconsistent with the character of this God. Abraham's God. *Our God.*

How did Abraham respond? Remember, we've seen that he had trouble trusting God with things that really mattered to him in the past. He took things into his own hands with Hagar and twice lied about Sarah. How would he respond now?

1. Read **Genesis 21:1–7.** How old was Abraham when Isaac was born? What does this tell you about God's timing when it comes to fulfilling his promises?

2. Read **Genesis 21:22–23.** What did Abimelek say about Abraham? What does this tell us about Abraham's power and position in the region?

3. Read **Genesis 22:1–2.** How would God's words have challenged Abraham's faith? How would it have represented yet another deviation to Abraham for how his future was going to play out?

Day Four: A Lifetime of Learning

We quickly learn how Abraham responded to God's call: "Early the next morning Abraham got up and loaded his donkey. He took with him two of his servants and his son Isaac. When he had cut enough wood for the burnt offering, he set out for the place God had told him about" (Genesis 22:3). *Abraham got up early.* No sleeping in. No trying to talk God out of it. No dragging his feet. Abraham got up, loaded the station wagon with firewood, took his only son, put him in the front seat, and followed God's navigation up the mountain.

What change had occurred in Abraham that he was suddenly so trusting of God? We get a clue in verse 5 after Abraham got to Mount Moriah and told his servants to wait while he and his boy marched on up the mountain. He said to his servants, "Stay here with the donkey while I and the boy go over there. We will *worship* and then we will come back to you" (emphasis added).

Ever since the days of Adam and Eve, people sacrificed animals to worship God. Abraham had sacrificed other things for God—like the comforts of his birth family and the country where he grew up. But this was taking things to a whole new level. Yet Abraham didn't hesitate. The next few verses tell us that he gave the load of wood to Isaac to carry up the hill while he carried the fire and the knife.

On the way up, Isaac noticed something was missing and pointed out that they had everything they needed except the animal sacrifice. Abraham responded, "God himself will provide the lamb for the burnt offering, my son" (verse 8). They got to the top, and Abraham built the altar. When the wood was all stacked and ready to be lit on fire, Abraham bound Isaac and laid him on top of the woodpile. The only thing left to do was slaughter his only son and burn his body. Here is how the drama plays out:

> But the angel of the Lord called out to him from heaven, "Abraham! Abraham!"
>
> "Here I am," he replied.

> "Do not lay a hand on the boy," he said. "Do not do anything to him. Now I know that you fear God, because you have not withheld from me your son, your only son." Abraham looked up and there in a thicket he saw a ram caught by its horns. He went over and took the ram and sacrificed it as a burnt offering instead of his son (verses 11–13).

What we see in Abraham's actions is that after a lifetime of learning who God is, he finally offered himself in obedience to his God. He stopped insisting that he would write his own life story. Abraham had learned that sometimes obedience requires sacrifice. And Abraham was willing to sacrifice the gift of his son, Isaac, because worshiping the Giver was greater than worshiping the gift he'd been given.

1. Read **Genesis 22:3–14.** What does the fact that Abraham wanted to worship God tell us about what he had learned about trusting God?

2. Why did God command Abraham to sacrifice his son? What do you think Abraham learned about God through this situation?

3. What are some things that God has called you to sacrifice to follow him? What can you learn from this story about putting your complete faith in him?

Day Five: Complete Surrender

As spectacular and as long awaited as his only son was, Abraham knew that God was greater. Abraham's obedience brought about a renewal of the covenant that God had made with him:

> The angel of the LORD called to Abraham from heaven a second time and said, "I swear by myself, declares the LORD, that because you have done this and have not withheld your son, your only son, I will surely bless you and make your descendants as numerous as the stars in the sky and as the sand on the seashore. Your descendants will take possession of the cities of their enemies, and through your offspring all nations on earth will be blessed, because you have obeyed me" (Genesis 22:15–18).

Abraham's story shows us that worship isn't something that happens in a church service. It's not singing songs or a genre we hear on Christian radio. Worship is about *surrender*. Surrendering to God's call to follow him where he leads. Surrendering to God's will when it doesn't match our own, or when we're too impatient to wait for him. Surrendering those things in our lives that we hold most important. And surrendering our personal story to live out our part in God's greater story. Worship is surrendering *everything* for the object of our worship.

Abraham's faithless encounter with Hagar and the lies he told about his wife involved him hanging on to something he shouldn't have. But his most faith-filled moments—leaving his father's home and his willingness to sacrifice Isaac—involved him letting something go.

What is your Isaac? What have you had to let go? Maybe it was something tangible like your dream car or that house in the perfect subdivision. Maybe you longed to have children and couldn't, or you envisioned staying home with your children but ended up having to work. Maybe you gave up your career for someone else.

Perhaps someone in your life has disappointed you and you fear you will never again have the happy family you desired. Maybe it's your opinion of yourself; you're so afraid of failure that you fail to live.

For all of us who hold on to things, people, or dreams too tightly, Abraham's story isn't a great piece of fiction to entertain us—it is *truth*. We are all like Abraham. He was a real man who lived, and sinned, and worshiped, and died, just like all the rest of us on our two-steps-forward, one-step-backward crooked walks toward intimacy with God. Abraham's story is about a real man's real encounter with a real God. And it's an encounter that Scripture invites *all of us* to have. No, Abraham wasn't perfect. But he learned to trust God, and as a result God used him to bless a nation and all of humankind.

He will do the same with us when we completely surrender our lives to him.

1. Read **Hebrews 11:8–12.** What acts of faith did Abraham and Sarah exhibit?

2. What does the writer of Hebrews mean when he states that Abraham "was looking forward to the city with foundations, whose architect and builder is God" (verse 10)? What does this tell us about what Abraham had learned about God during his life?

3. What is your "Isaac"? What is a dream or longing you have had to let go and surrender to God? How have you seen God work through your surrender?

SESSION THREE

When God Doesn't Fix It

It's hard to understand why sometimes Jesus heals and sometimes he doesn't. When it feels as though he's turned his back and walked the other way, it's hard not to be disappointed. Maybe even angry. But while we're focused on the unhealed sickness, hurt, and pain in our lives, God is focused on a bigger picture. . . . More than healing us physically, God wants our relationship with him to be healthy.

LAURA STORY

Introduction

"How are you doing?"

"Great!" "Fantastic!" "I'm too blessed to be depressed . . ."

Too many Christians are quick to give a flippant and often dishonest answer to this question. We feel that being "positive" shows the world we are walking in the joy of the Lord. We act like having faith in Jesus guarantees a painless existence.

But when we act as if everything is fine and cover up our struggles, we remove ourselves from honest conversations in the human family and slam the door shut on countless opportunities to talk about the presence and power of Jesus.

A woman named Karen was seeking to naturally share the love and message of Jesus with Sue, the woman who cuts her hair. Sue was kind but resistant to spiritual conversations. Any time Karen brought up church, faith, Jesus, the Bible, or anything that seemed religious, her friend quickly shut down the conversation. On a couple of occasions Karen had offered to give Sue a Bible, but Sue flatly refused to even accept this gift.

One day, Karen was getting ready to see Sue for a haircut but was considering canceling her appointment. She was in a time of deep personal turmoil and mourning, because that day doctors had called her with bad news about her daughter. Tests showed that her illness was back, worse than ever, which meant upcoming months of surgeries, pain, and uncertainty.

Karen made a decision. She would get her haircut, but she would act like everything was great. She wanted Sue to see her as a strong and faith-filled Christian witness.

When Karen sat in the salon chair, she was committed to having a joyful attitude no matter how she really felt. Sue looked at Karen in the mirror and tenderly asked this simple question: "How are you doing?" Uninvited tears flooded Karen's eyes and poured down her face. She forgot all about the facade she had prepared. Instead, Karen honestly expressed the raw pain and struggle she had walked through for more than a decade with her daughter. Sue listened with kindness and compassion.

Without any thought to what she was saying, Karen talked about her pain, sorrow, struggles, and also the presence of Jesus on her journey. Karen poured out stories of how people in her church had prayed daily for her family, how they had provided meals after surgeries, and how they had been family to her family. She talked about how God had used the comforting words of the Bible to minister to her again and again. Through her tears, Karen told Sue about the presence of Jesus, the hope of heaven, and the God-given strength she experienced, even when her heart ached and her tears flowed.

When her haircut was finished and her tears were all emptied out on the salon floor, Karen took a deep breath and thanked Sue for listening. Sue looked at Karen and said, "I think I would really like that Bible you offered me." That day, that moment of honesty, opened the door for a whole new relationship and level of spiritual conversation between Karen and Sue. The turning point was honest and unfiltered sharing of pain, loss, and suffering.

I grow more and more convinced that the greatest ministry any of us has to offer is to share our stories. It's through our imperfect lives, even our most broken chapters, that God's faithfulness is truly showcased.

Talk About It

To get things started for this third session, discuss one of the following questions:

- Christians often feel compelled to hide the hurts, fears, and life challenges they face. Tell about a time when you dared to be honest and transparent about a personal pain or struggle you were facing. How did the people you opened up to respond to your truthful testimony?

or

- If we share our pains and challenges honestly with other followers of Jesus, how can this encourage and help them on their own journey of faith? If we share these same stories with non-believers, how can this help them take a step toward faith in Jesus?

Video Teaching Notes

As you watch the video teaching segment for session three, use the following outline to record anything that stands out to you.

Our stories of imperfect lives and honest struggles can showcase God's faithfulness

When Jesus did not fix it

- Jesus displays his power and healing

- Jesus goes to a solitary place to pray

- The crowds seek Jesus and want him to come back and continue healing

- Jesus moves on to the next town and leaves many people unhealed

- Jesus is clear about what his main ministry was and what it was not

God sent Jesus to this earth not to make sick people healthy; God sent Jesus to literally raise dead people to life!

What has Jesus not fixed in your life?

How do we respond when God does not fix it?

The power of trust

What do we do when God doesn't fix it? We trust him. We trust that he is still in control, that he still is good, and that he still sees us and is near to us.

Bible Study and Video Discussion

Take a few minutes with your group members to discuss what you just watched and explore these concepts in Scripture.

1. Tell about a time God closed a door or slowed you down. How did this experience make room for you to connect with God or go deeper in your faith?

2. How has God answered prayers differently than you have asked or expected? How has God's timing been different than what you would have liked?

3. How have these experiences stretched or grown your faith?

4. Read **Mark 1:21–39.** Think about the day and night of ministry that Jesus experienced. What do you learn about Jesus as you watch him walk through this day?

5. How did the people of the region respond to Jesus' compassion and miraculous power? How do you think you would have responded had you been there witnessing Jesus' power to break spiritual bondage, heal fragmented bodies, and declare heavenly truth?

6. Imagine you had been part of the growing mass of people who gathered the next morning to ask Jesus to heal them. Imagine you had come to request healing in your own life or for a person you loved. What might have gone through your mind when you heard that Jesus was not coming back?

Is it possible that Jesus' top priority that day wasn't the physical healing of every lame and sick person in that town, but that his demonstration of power was only to reveal his greater purpose of spiritual healing to all of humanity?

7. In the video, Laura notes that times of physical healing might be designed to get people's attention so they can experience the spiritual healing that only Jesus can give. How do you respond to this line of thinking?

8. Jesus has power to bring physical healing. He has also laid down his life to cleanse us of sin and invite us into a relationship with the Father that will last for all eternity. When it comes right down to it, why is spiritual healing and faith in Jesus far more important and valuable than physical healing? With this in mind, how should this impact the way we pray and what we desire for ourselves and for others?

9. Jesus wants us to experience an abundant life. Sometimes this includes physical healing, but at other times it does not. What would you say to a Christian who declares, "If I can't be healed of a physical infirmity, then I can't experience an abundant life"?

As people of faith, we place our trust not in God's willingness to change our circumstances. We place our trust in God himself.

10. In the video, Laura talks about how thankful she and her family are for Martin's life. Although he still lives with disabilities, vision loss, short-term memory issues, and other challenges, she is deeply grateful and has a sense of God's presence and blessing. How is it possible to experience authentic joy and thankfulness in the midst of difficult circumstances? When was a time you encountered God in a deep way and felt profound thankfulness even in the middle of a life storm?

11. What are signs and indicators *we are trusting* in God even when we are facing pain and struggles and realize that God has decided not to fix our situation the way we want?

12. What are signs and indicators *we are not trusting* God and holding on to him during the times we face loss and struggles?

13. Tell your group members about a situation you are facing right now where you are struggling to trust God because he is not fixing the situation the way you had hoped. How can your group members pray for you and encourage you as you seek to grow in trust as you walk through this challenge?

God wants to restore our relationship with him more than anything else.

Closing Prayer

Use the prompts below to guide your group in a time of prayer together:

- Thank God for the times he has slowed you down or changed your course in a way that has ended up drawing you closer to him.
- Give God praise for times he has answered a prayer in a way that was absolutely right but very different from what you wanted at the time.
- Tell God that you are grateful for the times he heals physically, but celebrate the reality that spiritual healing is even more important.
- Pray for humility to accept God's sovereign and wise answers to your prayers, even when they don't make sense to you.
- Express joy to God for being with you at all times, even in the valley of pain and loss.

Between-Sessions
PERSONAL STUDY

Reflect on the content covered in this third session by exploring the following material from the Bible and from *When God Doesn't Fix It*.

Day One: A Shocking Healing

In the video this week, Laura discusses a troubling passage found in the Gospels in which it appeared that Jesus had the opportunity to heal people but instead turned his back on them and left town. It happened shortly after Jesus started his ministry and had chosen his disciples. He was in Capernaum, Simon and Andrew's hometown, and had just finished teaching in the synagogue. Luke writes:

> Jesus left the synagogue and went to the home of Simon. Now Simon's mother-in-law was suffering from a high fever, and they asked Jesus to help her. So he bent over her and rebuked the fever, and it left her. She got up at once and began to wait on them (4:38–39).

At that time, many people believed that a fever was an illness rather than just a symptom of another disease. They thought it was God's punishment for those who didn't obey his covenant. For this reason, only God could cure a fever. So the fact that Jesus healed her, and healed her so immediately, must have been astonishing. It suggested Jesus' divinity.

But let's not overlook *how* Jesus healed her. Simon's mother-in-law would have been considered a lowly old woman by this culture that didn't value women. Although Jesus could have healed her from a distance with his words, he instead chose to enter into her personal space and touch her. Using his bare hands, he helped her out of bed. In that small act, he demonstrated that God's love and compassion isn't reserved for the deserving, the blameless, or those with the highest social standing. Jesus cared for the least of these.

The miracle was quiet and private and took place inside of Simon's home. Yet the immediacy and completeness of the healing must have shaken the sails and rocked the boats of these former fishermen. They had never seen anything like it! The place had to be buzzing, and everyone who witnessed it must have been talking about it. Word quickly spread among the local community, and soon they wanted to experience it for themselves.

Luke goes on to tell us that at sunset, the people brought to Jesus those who had various diseases and who were demon-possessed. Imagine the scene. Just as the disciples are ready to retire for the night, a neighbor comes to the door and says they've heard how Jesus cured Simon's mother-in-law. Could Jesus heal them or one of their loved ones? Then a second neighbor, followed by a third, appears and asks for the same. Jesus obliges, healing each one. News of Jesus' healing powers spreads throughout the community, and soon the whole town is gathered on Simon's lawn.

1. Read **Matthew 25:31–44.** What does Jesus say in this parable about serving the "least of these" in society? Who are we serving when we serve these people?

2. Read **Luke 4:31–41.** How did Jesus demonstrate this principle of serving "the least of these" in this situation?

3. What cultural norms of the time was Jesus breaking by showing compassion to the sick and needy in Capernaum?

Day Two: A Glimmer of Hope

In Mark's Gospel, we read that Jesus healed "many" and drove out "many" demons (see 1:34). Luke tells us that "laying his hands on each one, he healed them" (4:40). Jesus didn't heal some and not others; rather, he healed a huge number of people with a variety of ailments.

Maybe like Simon's mother-in-law, some were there because of a fever. Others may have been born blind or with diseases. Perhaps they had wounds that needed healing. In that line could have been a man with headaches, a woman with an ongoing stomachache, or a baby with an ear infection. Jesus healed them all. A blind man, a deaf teenager, and an old woman with a bent back were now able to see, hear, and sit up straight.

Imagine what that must have been like. Formerly sick children were now running and playing as healthy children. Fathers who couldn't work and mothers who couldn't nurse were now able to provide for their children. Children with once twisted feet were now jumping for joy. Picture the euphoria these once ailing townspeople and their families must have felt as Jesus healed each of them. Grandparents weeping with joy. Parents hugging. Children yelling at play. Babies kicking and giggling. Sickness gone. Health restored. Jesus had fixed it all.

How proud Simon and Andrew must have been as they stood in front of their home listening to the joyful sounds in the starlit night around them. The townspeople must have gathered around the brothers to learn how they met this miracle healer. Simon would tell the story about the fishing trip where Jesus came walking across the beach. Then Andrew would tell the story of Simon's mother-in-law, and the townspeople would marvel. James and John must have walked through the crowd, astonished at what they saw and heard.

The townspeople finally left late that night, and Jesus and his disciples were able to go to bed. Surely the disciples slept soundly with smiles on their faces. They had to be so pleased with what Jesus had accomplished in their town and among their friends. That's exactly how we picture Jesus healing, isn't it? Completely. Immediately. Abundantly.

Maybe you've longed for this type of healing. Perhaps you have a disease, a physical or emotional pain that you have begged God to take away, but so far he hasn't. Maybe you have wounds from an abusive relationship, the death of a loved one, or some other painful situation you have endured. It could be that you prayed for healing from an addiction you can't shake, or an eating disorder that controls you, and yet you haven't seen the healing that the townspeople in Capernaum experienced. Though you've spent hours on your knees praying for a cure, for healing, for something broken to be fixed, nothing has changed.

Maybe you made it through a scary surgery only to find there are scarier surgeries ahead. The cancer is back. The disease is terminal. The paralysis won't go away. There's no diagnosis. There's nothing you can do . . . and God is silent. Your hope has dimmed because what's broken hasn't been fixed. But just when you're about to give up, someone says this can still be fixed. There is a new healer in town named Jesus, and he can help you. There in the darkest part of your night is a glimpse of a distant star called *hope*.

So you reach for the star and pocket it. And you go where that light leads you. To the specialist. To the new research posted on the Internet. To the rehab that guarantees results. To the therapist, priest, or pastor, who helped your friend. To lunch to receive the apology. To the bank for a loan. To the adoption agency. Or, if you lived in the first century, to Capernaum, to where a man named Jesus healed a town last night and where you hope to find healing.

1. Read **Romans 5:1–5.** How does Paul say we gain peace and hope in this world?

2. What does it mean to "boast in the hope of the glory of God"?

3. According to Paul, why should we also glory in our sufferings? How do the trials in our lives produce character and hope?

Day Three: A Bigger Picture

Continue to picture this scene in Capernaum. The news of Jesus' healing has spread, and now ailing travelers in the region are streaming into town. Swarms are heading toward Simon's house. His wife and mother-in-law draw water at the well for the thirsty travelers, as Simon, Andrew, James, and John look forward to what the day will bring. But there is a problem.

Mark tells us that "early in the morning, while it was still dark, Jesus got up, left the house and went off to a solitary place, where he prayed" (1:35). Jesus left town, and so far he hasn't returned. The disciples are mystified. Where is he? Doesn't he know what the day holds? Luke tells us, "The people were looking for him and when they came to where he was, they tried to keep him from leaving them" (4:42).

The peoples' expectation is that Jesus will return to Capernaum. But Jesus' response is not what they predicted. "But he said, 'I must proclaim the good news of the kingdom of God to the other towns also, because that is why I was sent'" (verse 43).

What? Didn't Jesus see the good that he had done and how much more healing was needed? Didn't he realize this was the most vital thing he could do if he wanted word of his ministry to spread? Sick people were streaming in from nearby towns wanting what the people of Capernaum had received—healing. Instead, they felt their last, best hope, had turned his back on them and said, "That's not what I am here to do."

Like these people, it's hard for us to understand why Jesus sometimes heals but sometimes doesn't. It's hard for us not to feel disappointed when it feels like Jesus, our only hope, has turned his back on us and walked away. But the truth is that God is focused on a bigger picture. There is something else that is broken in our lives, and there are eternal consequences if it doesn't get fixed: our relationship with our Creator. God wants to restore our relationship with him more than anything else. Even though he loves us, he will allow us to feel the pain of this world's unhealed hurts if it results in bringing us closer to him.

1. Read **Mark 1:35–39** and **Luke 4:42–44.** What reason did Jesus give in these two accounts as to why he had to leave Capernaum? What did he say was his greater mission?

2. How would you have reacted to this news if you were the disciples? If you were the people who had traveled to Capernaum seeking the healer?

3. Read **Isaiah 55:6–9.** What does this passage tell us about God's ways versus our ways? What does it tell us about God's desire to reconcile himself with sinners?

Day Four: Faulty Intentions

Simon and the men who stayed at his house were obviously concerned when they learned Jesus was missing. Maybe they were also frustrated, or embarrassed, when Jesus left without telling them anything. After all, they would have faced the crowds of travelers who had arrived in Capernaum seeking healing and found that Jesus, their only hope, had snuck away under the cover of darkness. So, when Simon and the others went out to find him, it was to explain why it was in Jesus' (and their own) best interests for him to come back to Capernaum.

But the Gospel writers subtly question if their concern was for Jesus or for the damage their own reputations would suffer when they couldn't deliver what the people were expecting. In Mark's account, the verb he uses (*katedi xen*) implies hunting him down. The verb Luke uses (*epez toun*) implies a similar type of relentless pursuit. The men were eager to find Jesus, and we can only assume this was to capitalize on Jesus' fame. They wanted to use Jesus' growing popularity to perform more healings and to gain more followers. But they failed to understand why Jesus had healed those he did.

Even as Jesus healed Simon's mother-in-law, he dropped hints as to who he was and the real reason he was there. Scholars point out that the verb Mark uses (*geiren*) to show how Jesus assisted Simon's mother-in-law means "raised." It is the same verb Paul would later use in his letters to show how God raised Jesus from the dead (see Romans 10:9; 1 Corinthians 15:15; 1 Thessalonians 1:10). Long before anyone knew that Jesus would be crucified and resurrected, Jesus was already dropping breadcrumbs of his true identity and purpose.

The problem was that the people in Capernaum seemed to have no interest in Jesus beyond his miracles. There was no mention of them sitting at Jesus' feet and learning from him. There were no invitations for Jesus to return to the synagogue and interpret the ancient Scriptures so they could learn more about his mission. The people of Capernaum and the nearby townspeople were there not to serve Jesus but to see how Jesus could serve *them*. And for a hot minute, Simon and the other men had the same mindset.

But Jesus wouldn't be distracted. He wouldn't reduce himself to a localized guru or a mystical medical man. He was a man on a mission, and that mission was to preach the kingdom of God to the nation of Israel. He didn't slink out of town in the dark; he left because he needed to be by himself to provide distance from the crowds and the men who were hoping that he would follow them. He went to a solitary place to spend time in prayer reconnecting with his Father and to make sure he was still doing what his Father wanted him to do.

By the time Simon and the other men arrived, Jesus had recommitted himself to his Father's work, not the sideshow of the night before. He reminded Simon and his companions that he hadn't been sent to Capernaum to be a local healer: he had been sent to the world to be a redeemer. The miracles Jesus performed were secondary to his real purpose. They were a physical example of what he had come to do spiritually for all of mankind.

1. Read **Luke 19:1–10** and **Matthew 9:9–13.** How did Jesus again break with social norms in these situations by serving "the least of these"?

2. What type of "healing" did Jesus provide to Zacchaeus and Matthew?

3. From these passages, what can we determine was Jesus' ultimate purpose and mission for coming to this earth?

Day Five: The Eternal Picture

The people waiting for healing in Capernaum understood the fall. Many of them were suffering the consequences of it, and they were waiting for a redeemer and rescuer. But when Jesus showed up, they hadn't yet picked up on all the hints that God had been dropping for centuries from the prophets. They hadn't seen Jesus predict his own death and resurrection, let alone actually go through it. So, of course, they were disappointed. They wanted restoration without redemption. But Jesus wanted them to see the full picture. He wanted them to see that he was the Christ, the Messiah, the Savior who had come to restore their relationship to his Father.

Yes, Jesus could have given them physical healing, but he wanted much more for them. He wanted to rescue them from *all* the consequences of sin and release them from the eternal punishment of their rebelliousness. He was God's representative on earth and had only a short time to reach as many people as he could. He also needed to train his disciples to carry on his message of rescue and redemption after he had left the earth.

In the end, we don't want a God whom we can push around. We don't want to be like the people who came to Capernaum looking for how God would serve them. We want the bigger the picture—the eternal picture. We want a God who can crush sin and evil with his foot. We want a rescuer who can reintroduce us to the God whom we've rebelled against. As much as we want physical healing, we want spiritual healing for our souls even more.

Each of us has broken things in our lives here on earth. Maybe, one day, God will fix those things, or maybe he won't. But the key for us to remember is that Jesus came into this world to bring true healing between us and God. Even when it doesn't seem that God will rescue us from what is broken in our physical lives, we can be assured that Jesus has rescued us from what is broken in our spiritual lives. He has created a way for us to not get what we deserve. He has created a path of forgiveness back to his Father.

That was his true purpose for coming to dwell among us, and the greatest gift possible that God could ever give to us.

1. Read **Luke 24:13–35.** What did the two disciples on the road to Emmaus say about Jesus? How had their hopes been dashed?

2. How did Jesus reveal the "full picture" to them? How did they respond when they realized it had been the resurrected Jesus in their midst?

3. What hope can you gain from the fact that even though God might not rescue you from what is broken in your physical life, he has already rescued you from what was broken in your spiritual life and your relationship with him?

SESSION FOUR

Why? The Question on Replay

We have to come to a point where we say, "I don't know why my life looks this way. But I don't have to understand why. It's enough for me to believe that God has a plan and that he has promised he will never leave or forsake me, and he will be by my side through every trial I face." I know this counters everything we think we want, but there is freedom in not having all of the answers—especially the answer to why.

LAURA STORY

Introduction

From the toddler years to the final days of our journey through this life, the question rings out . . . "Why?" It seems natural, just like breathing. We don't have to work at asking this question. It is on the tip of our tongue every time life brings a challenge.

A child is confused because Daddy and Mommy fight with each other. She asks, "Why are you yelling? Why are you mad? Why did Daddy leave? Why can't you love each other? Why can't we be a family?" The pain of relational conflict unleashes a series of whys in this girl's mind, and most of them don't lead to answers that make sense or heal her young heart.

A teenager is heartbroken because his girlfriend, his first love, no longer calls, drops by, or pays attention to him at school. "Why don't you love me? Why do you avoid me? Why are your eyes cold when you look at me? Why is my world upside down and my heart aching?" The sorrow of unrequited love, even adolescent puppy love, breaks loose an avalanche of whys, and most of them never find an answer that makes sense or satisfies.

A successful business leader shows up to work and is shocked to find out that his position has been eliminated in a corporate downsizing process. He is unsure of what to do next or how he will support his family. "Why my position? Why me? Why now? Why would God allow this?" The shocking news of unexpected life change elicits reflexive whys.

After forty years of raising kids, doing hard work, building a family, and caring for one another, a couple is looking forward to their retirement years. Both husband and wife share dreams of travel, long walks together, time to enjoy grandchildren, and a grand season of a slower pace of life. Then a doctor's report changes everything. With one word, *cancer*, all of their plans change. Why? A hundred whys!

Every season of life has moments of pain and loss. Every time we face the reality of struggle and suffering, the questions seem to begin with one word, one syllable, three letters . . . *why*?

Is it possible that rather than getting stuck for too long in our "why" questions, God desires for us to change those "why" questions to "how" questions? How might God's glory be best displayed through our struggle?

Talk About It

To get things started for this fourth session, discuss one of the following questions:

- As you think back over your life, what are some of the "why" questions you have asked that never seemed to have an answer?

or

- How can asking "why" be helpful and a valuable process? How can fixating on asking "why" questions become a dead end and an unhealthy practice?

Video Teaching Notes

As you watch the video teaching segment for session four, use the following outline to record anything that stands out to you.

When we are honest with ourselves, we all have our own "why" questions

Jesus' encounter in the Gospel of John with a man born blind

- The cultural shame in which he lived (bad theology)

- This same poor theology exists today

- Brokenness exists because sin entered the world

- The glory of God can be revealed through our brokenness

Even though God never promises us we will get all our questions answered this side of heaven, he does promise that every broken chapter of our story finds its greater purpose in his story of redemption.

Paul's "thorn in the flesh" and God's sufficient grace

God's greater plan for us

Changing our "why" questions to "how" questions

Bible Study and Video Discussion

Take a few minutes with your group members to discuss what you just watched and explore these concepts in Scripture.

1. If you could have an hour-long conversation with God, what are some "why" questions you would ask? How do you think having the answers to those questions would impact your life?

2. Read **John 9:1–12** and **9:35–39.** In light of these verses, what do we learn about how people with physical infirmities were viewed in Jesus' day? How might such thinking have impacted those who were blind or who suffered from other illnesses?

3. What do you learn from Jesus' actions and words in John 9? How does Jesus use this difficult and painful situation to bring glory to God?

God is good and is unable to be anything but good and perfect in all of his ways. And, God is sovereign.

4. What are some subtle ways that we, or others, can send the message that suffering, pain, sickness, and loss are a result of personal sin or a lack of faith? What can we do to combat these unhelpful messages?

5. How would you respond to a church leader who told you or a friend that your suffering was a result of sin in your life? What biblical evidence and teaching could you share that would combat this errant and unbiblical theology?

6. Suffering and sickness are not an automatic result of our personal sins, but sickness and much of the brokenness in the world are a result of sin coming into the world. What is the difference between these two statements: (1) "You are sick because of some hidden sin in your life," and (2) "Sickness exists because sin came into the world"?

"Just as sin reigned in death, so also grace might reign through righteousness to bring eternal life through Jesus Christ our Lord" (Romans 5:21).

7. Jesus was clear that the blindness the man experienced could be used for the glory of God. How can God use our brokenness, loss, and even sickness for his glory?

8. When was a time in your life that God used some experience of suffering or pain to bring glory to himself? How can your testimony lead others to God?

God doesn't allow his children to walk through any pain that he hasn't already predestined for a purpose.

9. Read **2 Corinthians 12:7–10.** How did the apostle Paul view his "thorn in the flesh"? How was God glorified and at work in the life of Paul even through his suffering and pain?

10. Tell about a time you faced a deep pain or struggle. Respond to one of the questions below:

    - How was God's glory displayed through your struggle?

    - How was God's strength revealed through your weakness?

    - How did you learn about God's sustaining power when your power ran out?

- How did you experience God's overwhelming peace in the midst of your difficult circumstances?

- How did your experience of anguish and heartache move you to think more about eternity, the life to come, and how you can live *this* day for *that* day?

Is it possible that God has a greater plan for our lives than fixing all our present problems?

11. Think about your own suffering, struggles, sickness, loss, or pain. What might happen if you moved from "why" questions to "how" questions? How might your outlook and disposition toward suffering change if you asked each of these questions?

    - How might God's glory be best displayed through my struggle?

    - How might God's strength be revealed through my weakness?

- How might I learn of God's sustaining power when my own shear fortitude comes to an end?

- How might I experience God's overwhelming peace in the midst of my jarring circumstances?

- How might the anguish and heartache of this life push me to think more about eternity and to more passionately live *this* day for *that* day?

God lifts our head and points us to hope.

Closing Prayer

Use the prompts below to guide your group in a time of prayer together:

- Thank God for loving you and for being patient when you ask your "why" questions.

- Praise God that he offers grace for your sins through the cross rather than holding your sins against you.

- Ask God to be glorified and lifted up in every experience of your life, including the times of pain, loss, and struggle.

- Invite the Holy Spirit to teach you to ask lots of "how" questions when you hit the rough times in life.

- Lift up your group members who are going through painful times and pray for them to experience God's all-sufficient grace along the way.

Between-Sessions
PERSONAL STUDY

Reflect on the content covered in this fourth session by exploring the following material from the Bible and from *When God Doesn't Fix It.*

Day One: Darkness and Light

In the video this week, we saw that the disciples asked Jesus a "why" question when they saw a man who had been blind from birth: "Rabbi, who sinned, this man or his parents, that he was born blind?" (John 9:1). In asking this question, the disciples were drawing on an assumption in their culture that physical ailment was a punishment for sin. Jesus responded to their "why" question by showing *how* God would be glorified through the man's condition: "This happened so that the works of God might be displayed in him" (verse 3).

Just a few chapters later in John, we find another story in which Jesus again shows a greater purpose for suffering and how it can be used to glorify God. This time, the afflicted person was one of Jesus' own personal friends. At the time, Jesus was traveling with his disciples when he received word from Martha and Mary, two sisters in Bethany, that their brother, Lazarus, was very sick. The sisters knew Jesus was a healer, and the implication in their message was that they wanted Jesus to come to them. So how does Jesus respond?

> When he heard this, Jesus said, "This sickness will not end in death. No, it is for God's glory so that God's Son may be glorified through it." Now Jesus loved Martha and her sister and Lazarus. So when he heard that Lazarus was sick, he stayed where he was two more days (John 11:4–6).

Huh? Even a cursory reading of this passage doesn't make sense. We know that Jesus healed the sick, and John tells us in his Gospel that he loved these people. So why wouldn't he immediately head to their home in Bethany to see how he could help? Bethany was a small village outside of Jerusalem. Was he avoiding Jerusalem for some reason? Was he scared to return?

In John 11:8–10, we learn that political tensions had been increasing in Jerusalem. The disciples tactfully reminded Jesus the last time he was there, the Jewish leaders had tried to stone him. There was genuine concern on their part that if Jesus returned to Bethany, they might all be put to death. So it seems reasonable to think that fear might stop Jesus from going near Jerusalem. But Jesus is the Son of God, so why would that scare him? And why, two days later when nothing had changed politically, did Jesus tell them they were going back to Bethany?

The disciples were certainly nervous about this announcement, and they questioned Jesus as to the wisdom of going back. Jesus' response didn't seem to answer their concerns. Rather, he made several confusing statements about how it was easier to walk in the light of day than in the dark of night. The group would most likely have been traveling during the day, so the comment seemed irrelevant.

Unless Jesus wasn't talking about day and night. Or light and dark in a tangible sense. Could those references mean something else?

1. Read **John 11:1–10.** What did Jesus say about Lazarus's sickness? What did he say would be revealed to the people through this illness?

2. Jesus' answer to the disciples' fears about his safety reveals that he knew his "twelve hours of daylight"—his time for ministry—was not yet fulfilled, so his life would not be extinguished until that time had come. What did Jesus add about those who also walked in his light—and those who did not?

3. Read **Matthew 5:14–16.** What commission did Jesus give to the disciples in these verses? How does this relate to what he told them in John 11:9–10?

Day Two: Missing the Point

As if Jesus' statement about darkness and light wasn't confusing enough for the disciples, he went on to tell them that Lazarus wasn't *dead* but was merely *sleeping*. Imagine how that statement must have set with the disciples. I can hear them whispering to each other, "We're going to wake up a friend of Jesus' who lives in enemy territory just because he forgot to set his alarm clock?" On the other hand, the news that Lazarus was sleeping gave them the support they needed to stay away. "Let him sleep! He'll get better if he gets his rest," they responded.

Earlier in his Gospel, John records a conversation that Jesus had with a Samaritan woman at a well. During that conversation, the Samaritan woman thought Jesus was talking about drinking the water in the well. But in fact, he was talking about spiritual water—living water—that would fill her so she would be thirsty no more (see John 4).

There is similar confusion in this passage. Jesus knew Lazarus was dead, but he also knew there was life after death. He tried to explain this foreign concept to the disciples, using terms like "sleeping," so they could comprehend what he was saying. But like so many who heard Jesus, the disciples completely missed the meaning of what he was saying. The only thing they understood was that a threat awaited them in Jerusalem—and they were afraid.

As Jesus walked ahead of them with purpose, they begrudgingly followed a few feet behind, whining about why they had to go to Bethany. Finally, Jesus had to spell it out for them. "So then he told them plainly, 'Lazarus is dead, and for your sake I am glad I was not there, so that you may believe. But let us go to him'" (John 11:14–15).

Can you imagine the confusion? They all knew Lazarus. He was a good friend. In Mary and Martha's message to Jesus, they had referred to him as "the one you love" (verse 3). So why would Jesus be *glad* for their sake that he wasn't there when Lazarus died? At this point, the disciples were likely too dumbfounded to ask any more questions. Instead, they silently trudged behind Jesus, bound for Bethany. And Martha was there to meet them when they arrived.

1. Read **John 11:11–16.** How do the disciples show their reluctance to return to Bethany? How did Thomas encourage the others to continue on with Jesus?

2. Why do you think Jesus said he was *glad* for the disciples' sake that he was not with Lazarus when he had died?

3. What does Jesus' delay in returning to Bethany tell us about his greater purpose in our lives? What does it tell us about apparent delays to answers to our own prayers?

Day Three: The Why Question

As Jesus and the disciples arrived at the outskirts of Bethany, Martha greeted them with the news that Lazarus had been dead and buried in a tomb for four days. From this chronology, we can assume that Lazarus likely died right after the sisters sent the message to Jesus. The messenger took a day to get it to him, Jesus stayed where he was for two more days, and then it took Jesus a day to get back to Bethany. As Martha pointed out, Jesus had arrived much too late to do Lazarus any good.

Understandably, Martha wanted to know *why* Jesus delayed. She told Jesus that if only he had been there, Lazarus would not have died. But she revealed that she still had faith in him: "But I know that even now God will give you whatever you ask" (John 11:22). Jesus replied that her brother would rise again, to which Martha answered, "I know he will rise again in the resurrection at the last day" (verse 24).

Once again, we see that Jesus was talking about something the listener didn't understand. Like most Jews who lived during Jesus' time, Martha believed there would be a resurrection at the last day.

She thought she understood what Jesus was talking about, but she was about to find out that she really didn't understand him at all.

Jesus tried to explain it by saying the resurrection isn't something that happens; it is a *person*. He said that *he* was the resurrection. And *he* was the life. He was trying to make it clear to Martha that it wasn't her belief in the *idea* of the resurrection that would save her from death, but belief in *him* that saves from death. This was such a critical message that Jesus wanted to make sure she understood it and asked her if she believed it.

As most of us would, Martha said she did. But how could someone grasp such a hard concept, especially someone who had never been exposed to it? And how could she foresee what that would mean for Lazarus? She had to actually *experience* the lesson to move her head knowledge to her heart.

When Martha went and got her sister, Mary, we see almost the same scene replayed, except that Mary had brought a crowd with her. The sisters again expressed their disappointment that Jesus had not come in time to save their brother. They believed that if Jesus had shown up earlier, their brother wouldn't have died.

Have you ever felt that way? If only Jesus had come when you called, you wouldn't have cancer. You'd still have your job. You never would have gotten in that accident. The recovery would have helped you stay sober. The addiction would be gone. The baby wouldn't have died. *If only* Jesus had answered your prayers, and done what you asked, when you asked.

Reading this far in the passage, we can't understand why Jesus waited two days before returning to Bethany. Just as we sometimes operate with an internal clock that betrays standard time, Jesus operates with an eternal clock. While we don't understand or always approve of how it works, his clock always keeps perfect time. He doesn't punch in and out according to our whims or our prayers. Our urgency doesn't increase or slow his pace. His timing is flawless—in the best sense of the word—and he sticks to it, regardless of how much we pressure him to do otherwise.

Jesus shows us again that he focused on something more than physical healing. He was about to answer the sisters' "why" question by showing *how* this tragedy would glorify God.

1. Read **John 11:17–32.** Martha could not understand why Jesus had delayed in coming to see Lazarus. In spite of this, how did she demonstrate her faith in Christ?

2. What "head knowledge" did Martha have concerning the resurrection? How did Jesus attempt to change her thinking?

3. In what ways have you felt like Mary and Martha when it seems your prayers to God have gone unanswered? What hope can you gain from their story?

Day Four: The Enemy of Death

What John tells us happens next is critical to understanding what Jesus was trying to communicate to Martha. Yet we need to read it carefully, as once again, it is easy to superficially look at the words and miss the real meaning behind what was going on. "When Jesus saw her weeping, and the Jews who had come along with her also weeping, he was deeply moved in spirit and troubled" (John 11:33).

The Jewish mourners were struck by Jesus' emotion. He seemed truly upset. Imagine how much comfort it must have brought to the mourners to see Jesus so moved that he wept. But *why* would Jesus be crying for Lazarus? Jesus knew what was about to happen. In fact, he had announced to his disciples days earlier that Lazarus was only "sleeping."

Here again, John is trying to tell us there is more going on in this scene than what we initially observe. When we look at the original language, we can see the English translation leaves us with a false sense of what was happening. For example, when we hear that Mary and the others were weeping, we might imagine a quiet, tearful scene. But the original verb (*klaio*) describes a loud wailing. Imagine a boisterous display of public grief, possibly with paid mourners to help lead the others. John suggests there were a great number of mourners grieving, perhaps due to Lazarus's prominent status in the community.

Jesus was certainly moved by their outpouring of grief, but the term "deeply moved" may not best express the Greek word John uses (*embrimaomai*). Instead, some biblical scholars translate it that Jesus was "warning sternly" or "angered" in his spirit and perturbed by the actions of the people. So, why was Jesus upset, and with whom?

Some have suggested Jesus was angry at death itself, and that is certainly plausible. Here was death in all of its pageantry, with crowds dressed in funeral clothes wailing and weeping. Jesus was standing before them as the antidote to death, but they failed to see that. *He* was the resurrection. *He* was the life. Yet the crowds questioned his powers. "Some of them said, 'Could not he who opened the eyes of the blind man have kept this man from dying?'" (John 11:37). Jesus, the only one with the power over death, was not recognized for who he was and what he could do.

When Jesus ordered the stone to be removed from the tomb, Martha replied, "But Lord . . . by this time there is a bad odor, for he has been there four days" (verse 39). The English translation sort of neutralizes Martha's comment. Essentially she was saying, "He stinks!"

The Jews believed the spirit hovered near a body for up to three days, until the skin lost its color, and then it was locked out. Jewish mourners actually checked on the body on the third day to make sure the person was truly dead. No one would dare take a look after the third day because the stench from the decomposing body would be overwhelming. In addition, there were strict purification laws about the handling of dead bodies. This is why they always buried the person on the same day the person died—just as they had done with Lazarus.

Martha's comment was meant to remind Jesus this was the *fourth* day—the check of the body had already happened, and Lazarus was truly dead! Without the modern burial techniques, decomposition would have started almost immediately, and she was warning Jesus that he really didn't want to go inside. In other words, all hope that Lazarus would somehow be alive was gone. Her brother was not only dead . . . he was stinkin' dead.

Jesus, however, reminded her of their previous conversation. He has just told her he was the resurrection and the life, and she had told him that she believed that it was true. Now he reminded her again by saying, "Did I not tell you that if you believe, you will see the glory of God?" (verse 40).

1. Read **John 11:33–40.** What emotions does Jesus express in this passage? Why would he have been angered and perturbed by the scene?

2. What questions did the onlookers ask each other? What does their response indicate about their opinion of the extent of Jesus' power?

3. What was the significance that Lazarus had been dead for four days? How did Martha express this concern to Jesus?

Day Five: Resurrection and Life

Imagine the scene! The crowds that had followed Jesus into Bethany now wait to see what he will do. Those who had been sitting with Mary look on in anticipation. Mourners who had been weeping near the burial place look up, confused by Jesus' appearance. Members of the community at the tomb watch warily, sensing something is about to happen.

They stand in a semicircle around the tomb, with Jesus at the center. Perhaps they have witnessed or heard of his other miracles. Some likely know he is in trouble with the local Jewish leaders. Whether they are for him or against him, no doubt they wait breathlessly.

Jesus steps forward and takes charge. With one look, several men come forward to do as he asked. They take away the stone. Then Jesus looks up and says, "Father, I thank you that you have heard me. I knew that you always hear me, but I said this for the benefit of the people standing here, that they may believe that you sent me" (John 11:41–42).

Then Jesus *commands* Lazarus to come out. Like a scene from *The Walking Dead*, this man, still wrapped tightly in his burial clothes, shuffles out. The crowd must have jumped back in awe, but also in fear. They whisper and shout to each other. "Lazarus is alive!" "Could it be?" "Lazarus lives!" They cry in joy and tremble in fear. Some fall to the ground. Some stare in disbelief. Others turn away, too shocked to comprehend what they are seeing.

But no one moves forward to embrace Lazarus. No one wants to be the first to touch the once-dead-now-risen man. Jesus must order them to take the grave clothes off Lazarus so he is free to go. At that moment, who cares about purification laws? When one man commands another to rise from the dead, and he does, you do whatever he asks! They quickly remove his grave clothes. My bet is that Jesus was the first to hug Lazarus—he was always the first to touch the untouchables.

What a miraculous event! It was too amazing to believe, but they had just seen it with their own eyes. John says that many of those who witnessed believed. But there were some who didn't. The real question is, *What is it that you believe after reading this story?*

Like Mary and Martha, we all have "why" questions that play in our minds when Jesus doesn't show up like we think he should. When his timing doesn't fit our own, we often conclude he doesn't hear us, doesn't care, or doesn't love us. But this story shows us that nothing Martha and Mary said or did could have changed Jesus' timing. And the only thing Jesus asked of Mary and Martha is what he asks of us. "Do you believe this?" (verse 26).

Jesus doesn't raise everyone from the dead, but he does raise believers from the dead to spend eternity in heaven with him and God the Father. We were dead in sin, but Jesus came into our lives and revived us, for he is the resurrection and the life. It is through our belief in him that we will see the glory of God, just as Martha and Mary did. And though he doesn't promise to restore everything on this earth in our time, occasionally we get a glimpse of things being revived. And in that moment, we see the glory of God.

1. Read **John 11:41–46.** What reason does Jesus give for performing this miracle?

2. How did Jesus ultimately answer Mary and Martha's "why" question? How would this miracle have moved their head knowledge of God to their hearts?

3. What were the two different reactions among the crowd who had witnessed the miracle? How does this mirror the way people react to Jesus' message today?

SESSION FIVE

A Better Broken

While our broken circumstances may not change, we can. We do this by clinging to Scripture, discovering who God truly is, being willing to share our story even in the trials, and looking for blessings in our brokenness. We are all broken, but we can have a better story. And a better story begins with using our brokenness.

LAURA STORY

Introduction

Some of the struggles and losses we face can get better. Sickness can go away. Financial instability can eventually stabilize. Relationships can be restored. Spiritually dark times can be followed by the bright presence of God's grace. Thankfully, some broken times do get better. But not always!

For Juan and Petra, the hope of "things getting better" was nowhere to be seen. While they were out of state visiting friends, a drunk driver ran down their daughter. They flew home not to watch their only child get better but to watch her pass away. No parent ever expects to outlive a child, to have to plan that child's funeral. There is no way to prepare for the devastation of such a moment.

This strong and Christ-loving couple was shattered by the loss of their girl. No prayer could bring her back; there was no simple declaration to make them feel better, no explanation for such random evil. Their hearts were broken, and the tears flowed.

More than a decade later, Juan and Petra are still married. They still love Jesus, still volunteer joyfully in their local church. And, yes, they are still broken, but it is a *better* kind of broken. Through the storm they have clung to God, to each other, and to their church community. They have wept an ocean of tears, and God has upheld them every step of the journey.

Even as you read these words, the testimony of their faith in the furnace can bring glory to God and hope to others walking through the losses and pain of this life.

Even when our situation does not change for the better,
we can change for the better.

Talk About It

To get things started for this final session, discuss one of the following questions:

- Think about someone you know who has walked through deep pain and loss that has simply not gone away. How has God been present in their brokenness?

or

- In what ways can God make us better through times of suffering and sorrow, even when we don't see an end to the pain we are traveling through?

If there's one thing I've learned walking through hardship, it's that it's futile to place our hope in the changing of circumstances.

Video Teaching Notes

As you watch the video teaching segment for session five, use the following outline to record anything that stands out to you.

Things might get better, or they might not . . . but *you* can get better

Place your hope in an unchanging God and not in changing circumstances

> Our hope must be found in something sturdier than God altering our circumstances in a way that's pleasing to us.

Three lessons you can learn from David's prayer in Psalm 40:

- An incorporation of your story

- A declaration of God's glory

- An expectation of the extraordinary

How your brokenness can find purpose in God's redemptive plan

The truth is that we all need Jesus

What it means to embrace a "better broken"

Embracing a better broken means that I'm not ashamed to be needy, to be broken, to be in whatever state showcases my desperate need for a Savior. Because the more I embrace my own inability to put myself back together, the more I can experience the healing grace of Jesus as he remakes me into the child of God he wants me to be.

Bible Study and Video Discussion

Take a few minutes with your group members to discuss what you just watched and explore these concepts in Scripture.

1. In the video, Laura tells a story about talking with a woman who had walked with her husband through a life-altering accident. Strangely, their intimate conversation took place in front of a radio audience. Laura says, "We spent an hour sharing our stories of God's faithfulness and provision." How are times of struggle and loss a powerful opportunity for us to experience God's faithfulness and provision?

Since God is with us during our trials, it is possible to have joy even in our trials. Joy is in the Lord.

2. Think about a time God showed up and provided for you in some surprising way as you walked through pain and loss. How did God reveal his glory through this experience?

3. At the end of the interview, the radio host told the woman, "I just know things will get better." However, Laura said, "I am not going to tell you things will get better. Honestly, it is possible that they might even get worse. But I believe *you* can get better!" How do these two statements reveal a different theology and understanding of what the Bible teaches about God and our suffering?

4. How do you think this woman might have responded to Laura's unique and honest declaration to her?

To get better in our brokenness, we have to replace the lies with the truth.

5. How do you respond to this statement: "Our lasting hope and joy must be founded on the unchanging person of Jesus"?

What are ways we can make sure our lives are not built on the shaky foundation of changing circumstances but on the rock-solid person of Jesus?

6. Read **Acts 16:16–31.** What were Paul and his companions doing that led to their being beaten up and locked in jail? How did Paul and Silas respond to the unjust suffering and abuse they faced? How is their journey a picture of a better brokenness?

Joy does not come from our circumstances;
it comes from our God.

7. Read **Psalm 40:1–3.** How is David's story and testimony woven into this simple song of trust and confidence? Given what you know of David's story in the Bible, how was he broken? How did God lead him and grow him through the times of pain, loss, and sorrow that he faced?

8. Share some of your story. How has God met you in times of brokenness? How has he made you better and more like Jesus through your struggles and pain?

Our joy must be found in the person of Jesus;
for that's the only thing in life that is truly stable.

9. Read **Psalm 103:1–2** and **Psalm 34:1–3.** While in jail, Paul and Silas sang out praise to God and gave witness to Jesus. In the midst of the pit and struggles, David still declared the glory of God. What are ways that we, with authentic hearts, can proclaim the glory of God in times of loss, sorrow, and pain?

10. Why are worship and praise difficult during times of suffering and hurt? Why are those actions helpful and necessary during hard times?

Things don't have to get better; we can get better!

11. David expected God to do extraordinary things. In Psalm 40:3 he proclaimed, "Many will see and fear the Lord and put their trust in him." In Acts, Paul and Silas saw the amazing glory of God as a revival broke out in the home of the jailer, and the jailer's family came to faith in the Savior. How can God do extraordinary things as we faithfully cling to him in our own hard times?

12. Think about a time when you clung to God through a painful season and he did something in you that would not have happened if you had not walked through the furnace hand-in-hand with Jesus. What did you learn from that situation?

13. The greatest example of a better broken is Jesus. How is his suffering for our sins and his sacrifice on the cross a perfect picture of undeserved brokenness that became an opportunity for God's glory to be revealed?

14. How can fixing our eyes on Jesus in the midst of our struggles help us keep the right perspective, attitude, and response to what we are facing?

15. As you wrap up this small group study, how can your group members pray for you, support you, and encourage you as you seek to hold to Jesus during your times of pain and struggle?

Isn't it amazing that no matter how far we run, or how deep we sink in the pit of our own destruction, God's strong arm of redemption always reaches farther? Praise God for this truth!

Closing Prayer

Use the prompts below to guide your group in a time of prayer together:

- Thank God for the times you seek his face in prayer and cry out in your times of need and he shows up and delivers you.
- Praise God for the times when the deliverance does not come, but the Deliverer does come and stands with you in your struggle.

- Praise God that in the midst of changing circumstances, his love and faithfulness never change.

- Declare prayers of praise and glory to God for his perfect love and sovereign wisdom.

- Ask God to help you see his redemptive plan even when you are suffering and struggling.

- Celebrate the amazing example of Jesus, the One who was broken and who makes you better, no matter how hard life can be.

FINAL PERSONAL STUDY

Reflect on the content covered in this fifth session by exploring the following material from the Bible and from *When God Doesn't Fix It.*

Day One: Unwavering Faith

In the video this week, Laura discussed Psalm 40:1–3, written by King David—a man who was no stranger to pain. This simple song illustrates three ways we can live out a "better broken." First, when David found himself in the "slimy pit" of misfortune and sin, rather than wallowing in it, he looked upward and allowed the Lord to lift him out. Second, rather than becoming embittered about the hard road he had walked, he chose to bless the name of the Lord. Third, he embraced his adversities with an expectation of the extraordinary. He looked forward to how God would display his power through his own broken story.

There is another man in the Bible who faced his own share of struggles, tragedies, disappointments, and pain, and also ended with a "better broken" story. The story of Joseph is a fascinating read, and if you've never read it in its entirety, you should. It's a narrative of a man who underwent significant trials yet remained faithful to God and was extraordinarily blessed in ways he never could have anticipated.

The story begins in Genesis 37. Jacob lived in the land of Canaan where his father, Isaac, and his grandfather, Abraham, had lived. He had twelve sons (and at least one daughter) through his wives, of which Joseph was his favorite. This angered Joseph's other brothers, who decided to sell him into slavery, fake his death, and tell their father that Joseph had died. Nice start to the story, huh?

Joseph was taken to Egypt where he was sold to Potiphar, one of Pharaoh's officials. Though he had gone from the comfort of being the beloved son to now being a slave, the Bible reminds us that God was with him. Soon, Joseph found favor in his master's eyes and was put in charge of Potiphar's household. That sounds great, until we learn that Potiphar's wife took notice of the handsome lad. She tried to seduce Joseph, but he rejected her, and she turned on him. Her lies sent Joseph to prison.

But once again, God was with him. Joseph found favor not only with his prison inmates but also with his prison guard. Though he was in prison for *years*, his faith didn't waver. During his imprisonment, Joseph was noticed for his ability to interpret dreams. Eventually, he was called on to interpret Pharaoh's dreams. His interpretation showed divine insight, and Joseph, despite his years of miserable circumstances, gave God all the credit.

It was clear to Pharaoh that Joseph had divine insight into the future. So Pharaoh put him in charge of Egypt to ensure that the country would survive the upcoming famine. As a result, they both profited greatly.

1. Read **Genesis 37:18–28** and **39:1–20.** What events led to Joseph being taken to Egypt and then thrown into prison?

2. Joseph acted with integrity in his dealings with Potiphar's wife, yet he nevertheless suffered the consequences of her wrath. Why do you think God allowed him to be thrown into prison even though he did the right thing?

3. How did God reveal that he was with Joseph *in spite* of the trials he was facing? What does this tell us about how God operates in the trials *we* face?

Day Two: Out of Control

Stop and think about the trials Joseph endured and the circumstances that were beyond his control. He couldn't stop his brothers from selling him into slavery. Even though he did the right thing with Potiphar's wife, he couldn't prevent her making accusations that led to his being thrown in prison. Nor could he get out of prison on his own. Even when Pharaoh asked him to interpret his dreams, it wasn't because Joseph had orchestrated those circumstances.

If you had no control over your circumstances, saw few of your prayers being answered, and witnessed your trials getting successively worse, would you have been as faithful as Joseph? Would you have still trusted in God? Yet we know God was with Joseph, and it was God who restored him. Do you believe God can do the same for you?

The story could stop right there, and it would be enough. Bad stuff happened to Joseph, and God restored him with a better position and with wealth, power, and fame. But God saw the broken relationship between Joseph and his brothers, and he wanted to redeem that as well. Once again, only God could make it happen.

During the famine, Joseph's brothers came to Egypt groveling for food. Joseph wisely tested their intentions before revealing himself as their long-lost sibling. Once he did, a grand reunion ensued, and they brought Dad to Egypt where they all lived happily ever after. At the end of the story, Joseph had gone full circle from beloved son and hated brother, to slave, back to beloved son, and now to the forgiving brother. But again, it wasn't Joseph who did any of this. God did.

God went on to use Joseph's trials to bring about redemption for his entire family and for the nation of Israel. God used Joseph to save the entire region from death by starvation. Joseph's role in this story was to be faithful, even during the trials.

But that's not all.

1. Read **Genesis 41:41–46** and **41:53–57.** How did God use the trials Joseph had suffered to prepare him to take command of Egypt? How did God use him to save many others?

2. What do you think would have happened if Joseph had turned his back on God during his trials? Who would have suffered in addition to Joseph?

3. In what ways was God working "behind the scenes" in Joseph's life? How may he be doing the same in a trial you are currently facing?

Day Three: All Worth It

God used the restoration of Joseph's family to bring salvation to *all of us*. For it is through Joseph's lineage that Jesus was born. Imagine that! Joseph suffered, yet he was faithful and trusted that God was with him. As a result, he not only helped save his family and his nation, but ultimately his faithfulness resulted in our salvation as well.

Were his trials worth it? His family would say so. The Israelites would say so. And we would say so. Though Joseph went through some pretty rough years, if we could ask him, he would say it was all worth it. How do we know this? Because even during his trials, he kept his faith in God despite the fact that he didn't know the outcome.

Would your trials be worth it if you knew the outcome? Are they worth it now while you're still experiencing brokenness? What could God be doing in your life while you're spending years in the prison of addiction, grief, or fear?

When we go through trials, it's easy for us to pray for such things as our protection, our health, and our own happiness. But God has more planned for us than those things we hold so close to our hearts. He's asking us if we'll still believe in him even if our life isn't comfortable, our days are filled with trials, our prayers aren't answered as we like, and our dreams die. He's asking us to have faith, despite our trials, because he has more good planned for us than we could ever hope for or imagine. As the Lord said through the prophet Jeremiah:

> I know the plans I have for you . . . plans to prosper you and not to harm you, plans to give you hope and a future. Then you will call on me and come and pray to me, and I will listen to you. You will seek me and find me when you seek me with all your heart (Jeremiah 29:11–13).

Just think about the plans that God worked through Joseph's trials. If he had abandoned his faith when he was sold into slavery; if he'd given in to Potiphar's wife; if he'd given up while in prison; if he'd lost hope when it seemed his friends forgot him; if he'd failed to forgive when his brothers presented themselves before him—then God wouldn't have been able to do the extraordinary things he did through Joseph's life and lineage. But Joseph *did* remain faithful, and each of us has been blessed as a result.

1. Read **Genesis 45:1–11.** The trials Joseph endured had come about not as a result of anything he had done but through the jealously, wrath, and neglect of others. In spite of this, how did Joseph see his situation? What greater purpose did he find in it?

2. What enabled Joseph to so completely forgive his brothers and want to provide for them?

3. Do you truly believe that God has "plans to prosper you and not to harm you" even in the midst of trying circumstances? What hope does Joseph's story provide to you?

Day Four: An Access Point

In 2 Corinthians 9:8, Paul writes, "God is able to bless you abundantly, so that in all things at all times, having all that you need, you will abound in every good work." In Ephesians 3:20–21, he adds, "Now to him who is able to do immeasurably more than all we ask or imagine, according to his power that is at work within us, to him be glory in the church and in Christ Jesus throughout all generations." God gives us blessings to help us do his work for his glory.

We see this principle demonstrated in the life of Joseph. His trials were part of a bigger plan that he did not see unfolding until years after the event. And some of the effects of his faithfulness he did not even witness during his lifetime. That's why our stories are so important. They're part of a much bigger story—God's story. While God doesn't always answer our prayers the way we would like, he blesses us abundantly and gives us everything we need to abound in the good work he has for us. When we do, our story, like Joseph's, will bring God glory because he can do immeasurably more than we ask or imagine.

Our brokenness is an access point into other people's lives. "I know what you're going through" is the only invitation we need to enter into someone else's pain. When people ask, "How did you make it?" we can tell them that it is only by God's grace we have survived. When we walk through trials, our example ministers more to other people than any compelling speech we might make. Our ministry becomes teaching others how we walked through loss, or through moral failures—someone else's or our own.

Whatever it is that we've come through, we can believe that God will use all of it—and then we can help others see how God will use their brokenness as well.

1. Read **James 1:2–4.** According to James, why should we consider it "pure joy" when we face trials of many kinds?

2. What is the difference between being in denial about our problems and seeing how God could be using them to do a greater good?

3. How have your trials enabled you to empathize with the trials others are facing? How have you been able to use what you've gone through to point others to Christ?

Day Five: A Higher Perspective

Near the end of Joseph's story, when his brothers and their families were all in Egypt, we read of the death of Joseph's father. Joseph mourned for Jacob and then received permission from Pharaoh to bury him in Canaan. Once the burial was over, and everyone had returned to Egypt, Joseph's brothers started to get nervous. "What if Joseph holds a grudge against us and pays us back for all the wrongs we did to him?" (Genesis 50:15).

So the brothers sent word to Joseph that before Jacob died, he had left instructions that Joseph was to forgive the brothers for the wrongs they had committed against him. When Joseph received this message, he wept and replied, "You intended to harm me, but God intended it for good to accomplish what is now being done, the saving of many lives" (verse 20). Joseph's statement demonstrates his ability to see the trials he had endured at a deeper level. His story, broken as it was, had led to the salvation of many.

It's interesting to note that God used Joseph even in the midst of his trials. We see this when he was in prison and interpreted dreams for the Pharaoh's cupbearer and baker (see Genesis 40).

When we're in the midst of a trial, we often think that once we're through it, *then* God can use our story. After we resolve our brokenness, we can use our story for him, because that's when we'll finally be whole and God can give us our next step in life. But the truth is that the next step after being broken is to allow God to use it. If we wait until there is resolution to our story, we'll never tell our story. Or, if there is a resolution, and our current trial has ended, another chapter or another trial will soon start. So choosing to wait before using our brokenness to help someone else is, in effect, choosing not to use our brokenness.

Hurting people don't live in the resolution of life. They live in the tension of a son who will never return home, a parent who refuses to see them, a friend who's betrayed them. Hurting people walk through the mess. They swim in the brokenness. And with God's help, they hope and pray to make it to the other side.

Simply put, that can also be your ministry. Your testimony can be telling people you're not to the other side yet. You're still fighting to get there. You can remind them that they aren't in their brokenness alone. You can encourage them to turn to Jesus—because he is the one who is sustaining you, and they'll never get to the other side without his help. On his own, the drowning man is weak. But when he looks to his Savior, even the drowning man has the potential to save himself and the others who call on his Savior. Knowing you've used your brokenness to save others from drowning in their trials is indeed a better broken.

When we take our eyes off ourselves and see how God has used us and our broken stories to minister to other people, we get to see what we were created to do. That gives us the true hope of heaven: knowing there is a Savior who saves us from this broken world and allows us to live in peace and joy for all eternity.

As the joyful guy in prison, the one with the thorn in his side, so aptly wrote: "For our light and momentary troubles are achieving for us an eternal glory that far outweighs them all. So we fix our eyes not on what is seen, but on what is unseen, since what is seen is temporary, but what is unseen is eternal" (2 Corinthians 4:17–18).

1. Read **Genesis 50:15–21.** Joseph had experienced many trials as a result of the brokenness of others, including his brothers that stood before him. At the end of his trials, how did he illustrate that he had arrived at a "better broken" place?

2. In 1 Thessalonians 5:18, Paul writes, "Give thanks in all circumstances; for this is God's will for you in Christ Jesus." How does focusing on the eternal instead of the temporary struggles of this life enable us to do this?

3. What is the "better broken" story that God has given you? How will you share that story with others to encourage them—even if you are still in the midst of a trial?

Small Group Leader Helps

If you are reading this, you have likely agreed to lead a group through *When God Doesn't Fix It*. Thank you! What you have chosen to do is important, and much good fruit can come from studies like this. The rewards of being a leader are different from those of participating, and we hope you find your own walk with Jesus deepened by this experience.

When God Doesn't Fix It is a five-session study built around video content and small-group interaction. As the group leader, imagine yourself as the host of a dinner party. Your job is to take care of your guests by managing all the behind-the-scenes details so that as your guests arrive, they can focus on each other and on interaction around the topic.

As the group leader, your role is not to answer all the questions or reteach the content—the video, book, and study guide will do most of that work. Your job is to guide the experience and cultivate your small group into a kind of teaching community. This will make it a place for members to process, question, and reflect—not receive more instruction.

There are several elements in this leader's guide that will help you as you structure your study and reflection time, so follow along and take advantage of each one.

Before You Begin

Before your first meeting, make sure the participants have a copy of this study guide so they can follow along and have their answers written out ahead of time. Alternately, you can hand out the study guides at your first meeting and give the group members some time to look over the material and ask any preliminary questions. During your first meeting, be sure to send a sheet around the room and have the members write down their name, phone number, and email address so you can keep in touch with them during the week.

Generally, the ideal size for a group is eight to ten people, which ensures everyone will have enough time to participate in discussions. If you have more people, you might want to break up the main group into smaller subgroups. Encourage those who show up at the first meeting to commit to attending the duration of the study, as this will help the group members get to know each other, create stability for the group, and help you know how to prepare each week.

Each of the sessions begins with an opening illustration. The choice of questions that follow serve as an icebreaker to get the group members thinking about the topic at hand. Some people may want to tell a long story in response to one of these questions, but the goal is to keep the answers brief. Ideally, you want everyone in the group to get a chance to answer, so try to keep the responses to a minute or less. If you have talkative group members, say up front that everyone needs to limit his or her answer to one minute.

Give the group members a chance to answer, but tell them to feel free to pass if they wish. With the rest of the study, it's generally not a good idea to have everyone answer every question—a free-flowing discussion is more desirable. But with the opening icebreaker questions, you can go around the circle. Encourage shy people to share, but don't force them.

Before your first meeting, let the group members know that each session contains five days' worth of Bible study and reflection materials that they can complete during the week. While this is an optional exercise, it will help the members cement the concepts presented during the group study time and encourage them to spend time each day in God's Word. Also invite them to bring any questions and insights they uncovered while reading to your next meeting, especially if they had a breakthrough moment or if they didn't understand something.

Weekly Preparation

As the leader, there are a few things you should do to prepare for each meeting:

- *Read through the session.* This will help you to become familiar with the content and know how to structure the discussion times.

- *Decide which questions you definitely want to discuss.* Based on the amount and length of group discussion, you may not be able to get through all of the "Bible study and video discussion" questions, so choose four to five questions that you definitely want to cover.

- *Be familiar with the questions you want to discuss.* When the group meets you'll be watching the clock, so you want to make sure you are familiar with the questions you have selected. In this way, you'll ensure you have the material more deeply in your mind than your group members.

- *Pray for your group.* Pray for your group members throughout the week and ask God to lead them as they study his Word.

- *Bring extra supplies to your meeting.* The members should bring their own pens for writing notes, but it's a good idea to have extras available for those who forget. You may also want to bring paper and additional Bibles.

Note that in many cases there will be no one "right" answer to the question. Answers will vary, especially when the group members are being asked to share their personal experiences.

Structuring the Discussion Time

You will need to determine with your group how long you want to meet each week so you can plan your time accordingly. Generally, most groups like to meet for either sixty minutes or ninety minutes, so you could use one of the following schedules:

Section	60 Minutes	90 Minutes
WELCOME (members arrive and get settled)	5 minutes	10 minutes
TALK ABOUT IT (discuss one of the two opening questions for the session)	10 minutes	15 minutes
VIDEO (watch the teaching material together and take notes)	15 minutes	15 minutes
DISCUSSION (discuss the Bible study questions you selected ahead of time)	25 minutes	40 minutes
PRAYER/CLOSING (pray together as a group and dismiss)	5 minutes	10 minutes

As the group leader, it is up to you to keep track of the time and keep things moving along according to your schedule. You might want to set a timer for each segment so both you and the group members know when your time is up. (Note that there are some good phone apps for timers that play a gentle chime or other pleasant sound instead of a disruptive noise.)

Don't be concerned if the group members are quiet or slow to share. People are often quiet when they are pulling together their ideas, and this might be a new experience for them. Just ask a question and let it hang in the air until someone shares. You can then say, "Thank you. What about others? What came to you when you watched that portion of the video?"

Group Dynamics

Leading a group through *When God Doesn't Fix It* will prove to be highly rewarding both to you and your group members. However, this doesn't mean you will not encounter any challenges along the way! Discussions can get off track. Group members may not be sensitive to the needs and ideas of others. Some might worry they will be expected to talk about matters that make them feel awkward. Others may express comments that result in disagreements. To help ease this strain on you and the group, consider the following ground rules:

- When someone raises a question or comment that is off the main topic, suggest you deal with it another time, or, if you feel led to go in that direction, let the group know you will be spending some time discussing it.

- If someone asks a question you don't know how to answer, admit it and move on. At your discretion, feel free to invite group members to comment on questions that call for personal experience.

- If you find one or two people are dominating the discussion time, direct a few questions to others in the group. Outside the main group time, ask the more dominating members to help you draw out the quieter ones. Work to make them a part of the solution instead of the problem.

- When a disagreement occurs, encourage the group members to process the matter in love. Encourage those on

> opposite sides to restate what they heard the other side say about the matter, and then invite each side to evaluate if that perception is accurate. Lead the group in examining other Scriptures related to the topic and look for common ground.

When any of these issues arise, encourage your group members to follow these words from the Bible: "Love one another" (John 13:34), "If it is possible, as far as it depends on you, live at peace with everyone" (Romans 12:18), and "Be quick to listen, slow to speak and slow to become angry" (James 1:19). This will make your group time more rewarding and beneficial for everyone who attends.

Also Available from Laura Story

In *When God Doesn't Fix It*, Laura Story tells of the unexpected turn her life took when her husband, Martin, was diagnosed with a brain tumor. Through her story, she helps us understand we aren't the only ones whose lives have taken unexpected turns. She examines the brokenness of some of the heroes of our faith and shows how despite their flaws and flawed stories, God was able to use them in extraordinary ways—not because of their faith, but because of the faithfulness of their God. God may not fix everything. In fact, our situation might not ever change or get better. But with Jesus, we can be better.

W Publishing Group

An Imprint of Thomas Nelson